SO-BYX-547

Invitation to the Lion's Den

by David Pierce
with Dan Wooding

foreword
by Rick Wakeman

afterword
by Floyd McClung

This book was printed by gifts donated in memory of
JOHN EDWARD CHAYA
born June 16, 1978
died January 21, 2000

Other Books by David Pierce

Dancing With Skinheads & Other Bible Study Topics, Steiger Press (1998)

Dancing With Skinheads und Andere Bibelarbeiten, German Edition, Asaph (1998)

Rock Priest, German Edition, Dynamis Verlag (1994)

Rock Priest, UK Edition, Kingsway Publications (1993)

Rock Priest (Rockowy Kaplan), Polish Edition, Wydawnictwo (1998)

For information, contact Steiger International, PO Box 1186, Northampton, MA 01061 USA; or visit us on the web at www.steiger.org.

David Pierce

about the author

David Pierce is the Executive Director of Steiger International, an international ministry of YWAM (Youth With A Mission), dedicated to reaching the "global youth culture".

Steiger means "pier" in Dutch and comes from the address of the barge where David and his wife Jodi started a Bible study for the punks and non-churched of Amsterdam, Holland.

Out of this ministry came the band, No Longer Music. Formed as an evangelistic tool to reach the secular music scene, the group has toured the globe since the late 1980's. Now, Steiger has ministry teams in Singapore, India, Serbia, Poland, Germany, Austria, England, New Zealand, and America

from false idols and religions and introducing them to the one true God.

Missionaries have been spreading the word in second- (communist bloc) and third-world countries for years now, of course, and long may their work continue. These people have a special talent which has been called upon and is being used in God's name. But for many years, with one or two small exceptions, this is as far as it's gone. The last ten years or so of this twentieth century have seen changes that must have surprised even the devil himself; but sadly, once he got over his surprise, he took control.

Drugs and prostitution have long gone hand in hand. Violence, satanic worship, crime and corruption are all part of today's world. Move this to Eastern Europe and mix it with atheism and communism, and the recipe is pure poison. The only known antidote is the Lord Jesus Christ.

But it is not easy to administer the antidote without a very special "doctoring." For this God has not only to select his chosen "doctors," but also to train them along the way.

David Pierce is one of these chosen.

His story is nothing short of astonishing. Thrown into a modern day lion's den, with little more knowledge than that it is the end without the tail that bites you, he entered a Christian — and emerged a disciple.

Nothing frightened him, except his fear of God. This comes through so strongly in the book that you can feel it transmitted to all he meets, both good and evil. He uses the power of prayer to enormous effect, whether it be on a crowded stage playing to many thousands of young people, on his own, or with his family. He is never ashamed to ask for help or guidance from God, and sometimes in an almost offhand way he shows the love he has for God and that God has for him. Various asides he has with God are really quite hilarious. For instance: "OK, God, if you want me to sing and dance in a really stupid way in this silly play, then I will!" Or: "If you want me to sing out of tune, then I'll sing out of tune!"

David goes where no sane person would even consider going, meeting with prostitutes, drug addicts, pushers, pimps, atheists, communists, Satan worshippers, Buddhist monks and New Age campers.

Throughout the book you will get the strong feeling that this is the beginning for David Pierce. This is his training. He has set up "churches" wherever he has been. The people who have been touched by him will never forget him, nor he them.

This is a book of achievement, attained by the power of God. Without such power and strength guiding him, this story could never have been told.

And what of the future for David Pierce? Well, all I can say is that if they ever do discover life on Mars, then I know who will be the first up there with a suitcase full of Bibles printed in Martian!

Rick Wakeman is one of the world's leading keyboard players and for many years was a member of the rock group Yes.

DANTE'S INFERNO

IT SEEMED LIKE WE HAD ENTERED the inner recesses of hell itself on that April night in 1990. Thick smoke enveloped the auditorium where we were to appear, making the hall in the Siberian city of Novosibirsk (pronounced *Noh-vuh-si-beersk*) appear like a giant ashtray.

The fires of free speech, fueled by Mikhail Gorbachev's *glasnost* policy, were just being kindled in this far corner of the Soviet empire, a city of 1,500,000 souls located at the junction of the Trans-Siberian railroad and the Ob river in southwest Siberia, and that small flicker was beginning to burn in the hall in an evil way that disturbed me greatly.

My band and I were backstage preparing to perform after a famous Russian "death metal band" whose "free speech" message to Siberian youth was that of hatred, death and suicide.

I had convinced two local pastors to come and join us at the concert. Earlier that day I had gone to their Baptist church and pleaded with them to stand with us.

"We are going to have a big concert in your city," I had told them. "Please come and pray with us. I believe that many are going to find Jesus tonight. We need you to help follow them up."

The dark-suited pair had eyed me suspiciously but after some discussion agreed to come and join us.

Backstage, our band was preparing for the coming concert.

Russell Archer, my California-born guitarist, who went by the stage-name of "Brussels Egg Furry," was pacing back and forth with his long mane of hair hanging down over his face, so you couldn't tell which direction he was facing. He was also wearing a long shirt down past his knees, so it almost looked as though he was wearing a dress over his blue jeans.

Our bass player, "The Captain," or John Sweeney, was also from America and also had extremely long hair, but not one strand was out of place. The Captain stood quietly, his lips moving in silent prayer.

Our drummer, Paul Versteeg from Holland, who we nicknamed "Klondyke," was wearing shorts and had wild blue eyes like a cat. As he strode nervously back and forth in prayer, he would bump into Russell.

I wore a pony-tail, and had on a sleeveless black shirt, a Harley Davidson belt and black tennis shoes.

The bemused pastors lined the wall, their eyes fixed disbelievingly on our band. When I sneaked a look at them, I could tell by their expressions that they didn't know if we were on their side or not— or even if we were from the same world.

Groups of crazed kids ran up and down the hallway, rattling our door as they tried to get into our room. Fortunately, we had posted someone there to prevent anyone entering.

As we prayed, I could hear heavy footsteps in the hallway. I knew it had to be Keith, because he walked like he was wearing flippers and his large frame caused earthquake-like vibrations. I stopped praying and opened my eyes. I could tell he was upset by what he had witnessed in the hall.

"Hey, you guys, we're going to need to pray really hard tonight. Those guys out there are *crazy,*" he said.

This disturbed me greatly because I knew that Keith himself was crazy. And for Keith to make this statement meant the audience must be really insane. We all began praying even harder. When you think you are going to die, you pray really hard.

It was time for us to go on stage. As I walked out, I looked into a sea of what looked like a thousand crazed demons. I soon learned that young people in Siberia know how to swear in English and also how to give the "finger". What a welcome we received!

I felt physically sick as I looked out at the staring eyes and frenzied faces. The crowd was wild and totally consumed with the death metal band they had just heard. They screamed obscenities at us.

As we set up our equipment, I noticed Keith off to the side with a cloth, and I walked over to see what he was doing. He gave me a look that indicated he was about to be sick.

"What's the problem, Keith?" I shouted over the noise of the crowd.

"I'm trying to clean this spit off your microphone," he said, beads of sweat appearing on his upper lip. I could see the thick and heavy spit. When he handed me the microphone, I could smell it.

It was incredible that Keith was with us at all on this tour. A year-and-a-half earlier, as a heroin addict, Keith had been living under a bridge in Amsterdam, eating out of garbage cans. Before Keith came to Amsterdam from the States, he had worked with many rock bands. He was on Michael Jackson's "Victory Tour" and was in charge of Michael's dressing room. He was part of the road crew with ZZ Top on the "Cheap Sunglasses Tour" and had eventually arrived in Amsterdam with Johnny Winter, who had recorded the musical backing for Keith to do a rap song called "An American in Amsterdam."

Keith had amassed a good deal of money during this time. He was living the high life in five-star hotels and was able to have all the things that money can buy. Slowly, he got deeper into drugs. He started off smoking heroin and then began to inject it. It wasn't long before all his money was gone and he began living under a bridge, eating from garbage cans, and supporting his drug habit through pan-handling and drug dealing in the Dutch city.

One day, while dealing drugs on an Amsterdam street, a young American wearing a baseball cap approached him and asked in a Southern accent if he could pray with him.

"Get out of here. Get lost. Can't you see I'm trying to do some business," Keith screamed angrily.

But the young American would not give up and every day kept coming back to talk with him, until finally Keith thought, "The only way I'm going to get any peace from this stupid guy is to let him pray for me."

"OK, go ahead. Get it over with," he snapped testily.

"But you have to be willing for God to change your life and to admit that you need him," said the young American, who didn't seem to know when to back off.

"OK, whatever," hissed Keith.

The American put his hand on Keith's shoulder. The drug dealers who were watching jumped back in terrified shock as Keith flew through the air. It appeared as if the young American had punched Keith in the face. But he hadn't.

"It was as if some invisible force had propelled me," Keith told me later. As he lay on the ground he felt a beam of energy go right through his body. "This energy was love!" he said. It was at that moment that he gave his life to God.

As a result, Keith became a great witness of God's power in Amsterdam. He also fell in love with a German girl there called Astrid and they asked me to perform the marriage ceremony. They soon became two of my closest friends.

One day Keith appeared in my home. All the blood had drained from his face, and Astrid's eyes were puffed and red.

"I'm going to die, that's it. I've got the AIDS virus," Keith told me. "I've just had a blood test and I tested HIV positive."

I was stunned. "Are you sure?" was all I could say.

"Yes, they tested me twice. They say there's no doubt about it!"

I didn't know how to comfort him and so we just cried together. I wanted to lift Keith's spirits so I invited him to join us on our tour of the USSR. I also believed God wanted to use him greatly on this trip.

I could see by the crowd that it was going to be a real confrontation, especially when we began to project the words of a song on to the screen in Russian. Our message was the opposite of that of the death metal band. One of the guys from our band spoke with their manager, who said he believed their concerts were successful when they got the audience to think about suicide. This was quite a contrast to our message which was of hope through God's love, and of how we need a relationship with Jesus.

I wanted to show that I was not impressed with all these crazy people and that I was definitely not impressed with Satan, whose name I could hear them chanting.

I decided to start the concert by singing a worship song, a cappella. This is not the normal way to begin after a death metal band, but I tried my best to sound like Amy Grant as I launched into, "I love you, Lord and I lift my voice...". I closed my eyes amid the screams of the crowd, and began to imagine beer bottles flying through the air and hitting me in the head. I shuddered as I envisioned someone jumping up on the stage and kicking me in the face with his heavy boot. It took all my courage to finish the song.

As I opened my eyes and our band started their opening riff, I looked at my microphone and I noticed a long piece of spit coming off it. Then I realized that people were spitting all over me. There are different things that you think about when people are doing this to you. The first is, *I don't like this.* The second is, *I wonder if I will get sick from everyone spitting on me?* So I tried to sing with my mouth closed. Finally, I thought, *Okay, God, if you want me to be spat on for you I 'm willing, but if you can get them to stop, that's okay, too!*

Through Tanya, my Russian translator, I said, "I have a message for you tonight. "God loves Novosibirsk." From that moment I felt God's powerful energy flow through the auditorium. Some people still laughed and mocked, though by now many also listened. We moved into another high energy song. Brussels Egg Furry obviously thought, *When they see how good I play guitar, they won't spit on me.* So he went to the edge of the stage and began a fast guitar riff. But those standing near him began spitting on him, too.

While all this was taking place, the Captain stood as far back from the edge of the stage as possible so that he wouldn't be spat on. This made me angry, because I thought that if I was prepared to get this treatment, he should, too.

Somehow the more they spat, the more compassion I felt for these broken and desperate kids. It was getting towards the end of the concert. I now felt I needed to say something. It didn't seem like the kind of venue where I could speak openly about Jesus, but still I knew I had to.

Common sense said that I should leave it there and allow the music and words to say it all. But I couldn't wipe the image from my mind of the time I had attended a U2 concert in Holland with some 65,000 people. During the show, every one was standing on their chairs, all their attention focused on Bono, the lead singer. It was an incredible experience to be with so many people and yet feel so unified. Someone who had spent time with Bono told me that he was a Christian.

I had thought to myself, *Give glory to God, Bono.* As I was thinking this, I noticed a beautiful sunset and rays of red tinged light began funneling into the stadium. *Give glory to God, Bono. They'll listen to you. You don't have to say a lot. Just say something.*

I kept hoping he would make a statement for God. But he didn't say anything. And everyone left the stadium singing, "I still haven't found what I'm looking for."

Even Prince and Madonna say "God bless you" at the end of their concerts, but Bono said nothing. So, standing on my chair in that stadium, I told God, "I know I'm not a great performer like Bono, but if you give me the opportunity, I'm going to give you all the glory." I decided that, even if it closed every door for me, I would always talk boldly of God from the stage.

So now I took a deep breath, and shouted, "Who do you worship? I know what you're thinking. You don't worship anybody. Right?" As this was interpreted, I heard some laugh at what I had said, but still I pressed on.

"You're wrong," I shouted back through a wall of jeers. "I know what you worship. You worship music. And the bands you worship don't even love you. In fact, they hate you. I know what you worship. Vodka. Yes, vodka," I continued. "I've seen people here waiting in long lines just to buy some."

"Yes, vodka," many screamed back, holding up their bottles in a drunken salute to me.

"Let me tell you who I worship," I pressed on. "I worship the One who made all the beautiful mountains around your city. The One who created the beautiful forests in Siberia. He created a world with clean air and good food. He wanted a good life for all his children.

"But we have turned our backs on him and say that we want to create our own system. After all, we say, God is only for old women. And so we create a world full of hatred and suffering and, because of this, sickness and death has entered the world.

"But this Father God is *not* weak. He's strong and he's powerful and he loves us. And he was not willing to leave us without hope. So he asked his son, Jesus, if he'd be willing to show us the way back to this good and loving Father.

"And when Jesus came, he did not drive a Mercedes or live in a palace. He fed the poor and he healed the sick, and he did not fit into our system. So we took Jesus and killed him. And we said, "Good, now we don't have to worry about Jesus any more."

"But Jesus was not just another man dying for another cause. He was also God's Son. And because of that, Jesus was stronger than death. He came back to life and rose from the dead and, because of that, I am not ashamed to say that I *love God.*"

Again I felt the supernatural power of God falling upon the audience.

"Many of you are empty inside. You have a big hole that you are trying to fill with many things," I declared. "Some of you can't go to sleep at night without drinking vodka or listening to music. Some of you think that money is going to bring you peace.

"But what you really need is Jesus. How can you know Jesus? Not by trying to make yourself better. There was a priest who went to Jesus, who went to the church every day and who tried to be good, but Jesus told him that wasn't good enough. He needed a new heart. He told this priest that he had to be 'born again.'

"There's only one thing that can separate you from God's love. And it's not the bad things that you have done. God can forgive you for any terrible thing you have done, because when he died for us, he took our guilt upon himself. Jesus said that we must become like little children. We must humble ourselves if we want to see God. Pride is the only thing separating us from this loving Father."

The audience had by now become very quiet.

"I'm now going to ask you to do something very brave," I concluded. "If you need to know Jesus, I'm going to ask you to come up here on the stage with all your friends watching and kneel with me."

I sank to my knees on the stage, and sixty young people literally fought their way through the crowd to join me there. People near the front were trying to block their way to the stage, but these courageous kids battled through.

As I led them in prayer, they echoed my prayer to all those listening in the hall, "Jesus, I need a new heart. Forgive me for the bad things I have done." I noticed tears well up in Russell's eyes as the young man who had spat on him knelt to receive Christ.

Many of those on the stage were broken and sobbing as they made their decision to follow Jesus. "From this night on you will never be the same," I told them.

We gave them some literature and linked them with the local Baptist pastors. These men now knew that we were on the same side!

As Andy Butcher, a British friend of mine said later, "You could almost hear the angels strumming their harps with joy. With plenty of reverb, of course!"

FIERCE PIERCE

IT WAS A TYPICALLY HOT and muggy summer's day in Brooklyn Center, a northern suburb of Minneapolis, Minnesota. I was preparing to stomp on a spider when I noticed a black funnel-like cloud ominously close on the horizon.

"A tornado," I shouted to my kid sister, Patti, who was ten years old and was playing on the swings. Misty, our border collie, was running backwards and forward as Patti kicked her legs with happy abandon in the sticky, humid air.

"Liar," she scowled, irritated that I would try and spoil her fun.

"All right, if you don't believe me, you can come and look for yourself," I insisted.

Patti got off the swing and walked towards me. Then she, too, saw it! The cloud twisted and rolled. Her eyes became big and frightened.

"Hurry, we've got to get to the basement," I said urgently, as the air moved, jerkily at first, and the cloud advanced like an army. I knew that I had to be responsible, because my parents were away shopping. So we rushed downstairs and hid under the pool table. There we were, my sister, my dog and my beloved radio.

As the tornado approached the house, I could hear the doors begin to slam violently to and fro from the pressure of the funnel cloud, sending a series of seismological thuds through my body. There was a quiver in my voice and an unsteadiness in my hand as I began to pray out loud. "God, if you save me from this tornado, I will never listen to rock music again." I clenched my fist until the knuckles showed white. What was I saying? Did this mean that I couldn't ever again listen to my idols like Eric Clapton, Creedence Clearwater Revival, the Rolling Stones, Neil Young and Bob Dylan?

The tornado lifted just before its full force reached our house, but our pet rabbit flew, in its cage, into our next door neighbor's yard. When we finally emerged, it was calmly eating the grass outside. The cage door had opened and it was enjoying a few minutes of freedom.

When I realized in this moment of post-storm euphoria that I wasn't going to die, I wiped the sweat off my face and I thought that God wouldn't mind if I still occasionally listened to rock music.

Burying my conscience, I would clandestinely tune into KDWB, the local rock station, but when I heard my father approaching my room, I would quickly switch to the Christian station, KTIS. He did not approve of my listening to rock music.

Bud, my father, was originally from Tacoma, Washington, and never knew his own father. His mother brought him to hear a local evangelist and it was then, when he was a little boy, that he made a decision to follow God.

Even at an early age, he was quite a character. When he was twelve years old, he wore a sandwich board which said, "Don't go to see [an evangelist who was coming to town], signed: The Devil." Dad would wear it into the rough bars in town and they would throw him out.

My father was a gifted athlete, and I greatly admired him. It was my goal to be a great athlete just like him. In my teenage years, he was the athletic director and basketball coach at a local Christian university.

Joanne, my mother, a local girl, made great sacrifices for all of us. She was always there for my sister, Patti, myself and second sister, Julie, who arrived some thirteen years after I was born. Mom was up at the crack of dawn to prepare breakfast for us in the morning, and she was there to ask us how our day had gone when we returned from school.

I was always the shortest guy in my class and couldn't seem to stay out of trouble. There was a boy across the street from where I lived named Loren Sin. He was the kind of kid who grew a full beard when he was ten years of age, and when I got on the school bus in the morning, the older kids would say, "Hey, Sin, Fierce Pierce said that he could beat you up."

This would incense Sin, and he would rush to the back of the bus and begin swinging at me. This painful ritual would take place almost every day on the way to school. Throughout junior high, if I could get through an entire day without getting into a degrading scuffle with somebody, I thought it was a good day.

My childhood was a far cry from that in the fictitious Lake Wobegon of Garrison Keillor. I was raised instead in a well manicured suburb of the "Twin Cities" of Minneapolis and St. Paul.

Every Sunday, my parents took me to Brooklyn Center Baptist Church. I would usually sit in the back row with my friends Mark Griffin, Tim Lane, Ray Teichroew and David Foy, or "Brillo Pad," as we called him. David was our role model. Although he was short and skinny and had hair like a Brillo pad and pimples all over his face, he taught us how to play practical jokes during the service. One particular Sunday the service seemed never-ending, so Brillo Pad put two pencils in his nose and another two in his ears and started making duck noises with his "duck call."

The Pastor stopped his sermon and let his eyes sweep the congregation for the perpetrator of the noise. We all watched in dead silence. I tried to make myself inconspicuous, but I finally couldn't suppress my peals of laughter and he fixed his eyes on me.

"David Pierce, be quiet," he said in a severe tone. My face flushed, and this public reprimand caused me to be punished by my parents: I had to wash the dishes for a week.

In fact, for my entire ninth grade, I had to do the dishes because it seemed like I couldn't keep myself out of trouble. It was as though there was something inside me, pointing me to trouble.

Three times a year my parents would go to Parent Teacher Conferences. I would work inordinately hard to be good the week before they would have the meeting with my teachers. But no matter how hard I tried I couldn't be good.

In one of my classes, the teacher tried to give an assignment and I got the whole class to chant, "No, no, no." He became the butt of my endless practical jokes which sadly would inflict pain and humiliation on him. So he would back off and wouldn't make us do the work. Finally, one day, he got so angry with me that he picked me up and tried to dump me head first into a waste-paper basket, but I was able to fight and kick myself free.

I think my endless persecution finally caused him to crack. One morning, as the students were coming into his class, they found him standing on top of his desk, singing, "Yummy, yummy, yummy, I've got love in my tummy!" He was hauled off to the local insane asylum for immediate and urgent care.

In my chemistry class I used to take a pair of scissors and heat it up with the lab-burner, so when people would take them out they would burn their hands.

More than anything else I really wanted to be a good athlete like my father. I would get up early in the morning and work late at night, practicing basketball. I even shoveled the snow off the driveway in the winter to practice shooting baskets but, because I was so short, when I tried out for the high school team I was never given a chance.

One day a friend told me that I should try for the school play, a comedy called "Mrs. McThing." So almost for a joke, I did. The teacher asked me to read the script and immediately gave me the lead part. I was surprised how excited my parents were about it, but for me it wasn't important because it wasn't sports. Because I was the youngest to get a part, the other members of the cast wouldn't talk to me and they didn't even invite me to the cast party. I didn't try for any more plays after that, even though acting came easily to me.

Drama was the one subject in which I was able to do well. I joined an advanced theater class in high school. But even then things didn't work out. In one particular play, I was to exit the stage after the one playing a king had given his speech. I was supposed to then close the curtain, but when the time came, I wouldn't do it—I just laughed at him as he tried to make up new lines to cover the confusion. This naturally made the drama teacher very upset.

Finally one day the teacher said, "All those who want to do serious plays, go on this side of the room and all those that want to just not be serious and to fool around like Pierce, go on the other side of the room."

Everyone went on my side of the room. It was then that I realized that I had real leadership skills.

EVERYBODY'S HOUSE

I WOKE UP SUDDENLY in the middle of the night and broke into a cold sweat. I immediately started reading the Bible that I had stashed under my pillow. I felt if I didn't the demons might get me. This strange behavior started one night after I received a phone call from my friend Scott. He had been hitchhiking back and forth across America while I was attending college. He didn't cut his hair for a couple of years and always carried a dulcimer with him.

"Hi, Scott, what's up?" I said.

"We've got to talk," he said in an agitated voice.

"Why, what's wrong?" I asked.

"I'm ready to give my life to God," he responded. He told me that he had discovered there really was a spiritual world of evil and that he was afraid of it and that he "needed to know God."

Scott said he had recently seen the movie *The Exorcist,* and it had given him a revelation of the reality of evil. He had been involved with transcendental meditation and had opened himself up to it.

I discovered that the main reason he had called me was an extraordinary incident that he had just experienced. He told me, "I was in my car with two friends who believe in God and they were stressing the importance of accepting Jesus soon because the time is short. We all have only a certain number of days on this earth and the world may end. As they were speaking, a poorly-dressed man who looked like his home was the street, stepped from the curb into the crosswalk, raised his left arm high, pushed up his coat sleeve so his watch was clearly visible, riveted his eyes onto mine and raised his finger to his watch and began tapping it. He did this all the way from one side of the street to the other.

"This was a chilling experience and a very loud, overt message that I took to be direct from God as both a warning and an invitation. So I drove straight home, picked up the phone and called you."

"We need to go see Pastor Churchill," I said. Pastor Churchill was the pastor of Minnetonka

Community Church, where my parents attended. Since I wasn't going to a particular church at the time, it was the best I could come up with.

"OK, whatever you think," Scott said.

Scott was on his way to a party where he was to meet Annie. She was two years younger than Scott, and he wanted to tell her what he was going to do. She said she had had some of the same kind of thoughts he had described to me.

"Can I come with you?" she asked.

"Sure," said Scott, and I picked them both up at the party and drove them to the church. That night they both asked Jesus to come into their lives.

After Scott and Annie prayed to know God, I, too, discovered the reality of God for the first time. Before that I believed there must be a God, so I took out my "hell insurance" and "asked" Jesus into my life. But the question I always asked myself was, *What can I do and not lose my hell insurance?* So I tried to live as close as I could to the world. It was during this time that my life was turned completely upside down. I discovered the incredible life there is in following Jesus.

For the first time I started to understand the Bible and to see strange things happen. One time, Scott came into my room and said he was really afraid. He explained that he would keep waking up in the middle of the night feeling the presence of a powerful and evil personality in the room.

I told him, "The next time this happens, speak to it. Tell it, 'I don't belong to you anymore, I belong to Jesus'." So he did and it vanished as he spoke and he never had trouble with it again.

Scott then asked me, "Can we meet together every week and read the Bible together?"

"Sure," I said. In my mind, it was going to be just Scott, Annie and myself. But to my surprise, when we had our first meeting in a house by the University of Minnesota, I walked into a room full of people, many of whom were the radicals from the university. Because I was the only one there with a church background, I was appointed leader. Soon the Bible study grew so big that there were people overflowing into the hallways and into the kitchen.

More and more of my time was taken up by this group at the university, so I decided to enroll at the university and major in philosophy.

Scott and I decided we needed a bigger place to meet. So we found a former fraternity house in Dinkytown, a neighborhood at 14th Avenue and 4th Street, close to the university. It was loaded with interesting retail stores, curiosity shops and restaurants of several nations. Together we signed a contract for the place and decided to call it "Everybody's House." We did this because we wanted to accept everybody without condition, even cult members who came to "convert us." We talked with them, with street people, the mentally deficient, glue sniffers, needle junkies, criminals, drunks, and all minority groups. Often we would have different nationalities and we eventually welcomed people from seven foreign countries and 45 states who came to Everybody's House.

The only rules were these: no alcohol or drugs. Every crazed, insane person from throughout the city seemed to find their way there. Occasionally, even a few "normal" people would come as well.

In Everybody's House there was a large room with a fire place; we would crowd into the room and I would give weekly Bible teachings. We became known throughout the university.

Most Christian groups and churches in the community shunned us because we didn't conform to their expectations of how a group of Christians should conduct themselves. But people who would never go to church came to our Bible studies.

At one time there was a man at Everybody's House who was trying to steal money and other things. When he was confronted by one of our residents, he began swinging at him, but he couldn't hit him because there seemed to be a "force field" all around him. The guy said, "I can't break anything in this house. I can't steal anything in this house. They won't let me." He then ran out. So I began to believe that God could move in a supernatural way. I even grew to expect that he would. The fear I had of Satan's power was replaced by a faith in God's power.

Periodically, we would hold giant parties at Everybody's House. We would hire a searchlight for the front yard, an Elvis impersonator for the living room and a Bob Dylan acoustic-type singer for the downstairs. We also would get lots of day-old food from a local bakery for free. We would set up tables for food. We would advertise all over the university about our parties and hundreds would turn up. We would have giant snake dances around the area and block the traffic.

On the west bank of the university, where the hard-core radicals would hang out, there was a coffeehouse called "Extempore." This place was notorious for all the anti-war and left-wing activists that would frequent it, as well as drug addicts. It was the most radical place in that part of the Midwest. In the restaurant you could pay whatever you wanted for the food. They even had someone there giving classes on "Why Jesus was a Fraud." Harold, the man giving these classes, and I later became good friends and had many long discussions together.

The guy in charge of Extempore asked me if I would come and have a weekly Bible study there. He really respected us and thought that I was a cool guy. He didn't see Scott or myself as outsiders. Often strange things would happen while we were meeting there. One time, a group of guys all dressed in black came in and began praying to "the God of this earth" to come down on us during the meeting. We just stopped talking, started praying silently, and they ran out, afraid.

Eventually, I was giving three Bible studies a week at different places on the campus.

One day I was walking through the university and I felt that I had a 10-ton weight on my shoulders. It was so heavy, I could hardly keep my eyes open or put one foot in front of the other. I didn't understand why I was feeling the way I was.

Then I came the closest I've ever come to hearing an audible voice from God. It seemed like he said to me, "David, I won't forget all the things you've done for me." I didn't understand why I felt God was telling me this, but I was about to learn.

When I got back to Everybody's House I went downstairs to my office to do some work. A peculiar feeling of foreboding hung over me but I wasn't able to pinpoint the cause of my anxiety. Suddenly the door opened and all the other leaders of our ministry marched into the room. I noticed that Scott was not with them.

"We want you out of this place immediately," one of them said, his voice quivering with anger.

I was stunned. "What did you say?" I asked incredulously.

"We want you out of here immediately," he repeated.

My tongue was temporarily locked. I took a deep breath and then let it out slowly.

"Why?" I responded.

An embarrassed look came over his face.

"Because we know of fourteen women that you have seduced," the spokesman continued in a sharp, accusing tone, a bitter edge to his voice.

"Can I face my accusers?" I asked my face turning scarlet with anger.

"No, you cannot," he brusquely snapped back.

The full impact of his words by now became clear to me. My head was thudding with shock and my nerves cranked up another notch as I grabbed all the things from my desk, emptied out my room, and half walked, half ran to my car and threw everything in it. Something inside me said, "Don't fight this."

As I drove away, I found my initial anger melting away and being replaced with honest questioning. I suddenly felt a twinge of remorse. Was I partly to blame for these allegations? It was true that I had taken out several girls from the university, though not fourteen of them. I had not had sex with any of them, but still God convicted me of my relaxed attitude when I was with them and I understood that I was guilty, not of what I was accused of, but of a cavalier attitude. I was a leader and should have set a better standard.

The entire ministry collapsed a week later. I began to wonder if this was a bad dream from which I would never escape.

This incident happened during finals week in the fall of 1977. I had not only lost my campus outreach, but now all my friends apparently despised me as well. I felt deserted and alone, and then I recalled the impression I had felt from God when I was walking through the university. Even though I felt like a total failure, I still believed I had a calling on my life, but I also had a feeling that I had blown it and that was it. There was no way back.

It was a feeling that came back to haunt me time and time again.

It would be some time before I could shake the dragging sense of bewildered desolation at a situation that I could not fully understand and that no one could explain to me.

EUROPEAN VACATION

4

"DAVID, YOU NEED MORE EDUCATION. You should go to seminary." This was the advice of my father shortly after I had graduated from the university. I hated the idea, but I still went ahead and was accepted into a seminary in Minneapolis, where I was planning to study for my Masters Degree in Divinity.

But before school started I thought I would travel around Europe for a few weeks. I knew it would be good to get away from the scene that had brought me so much pain. I longed to have some time by myself, seeing the sights of Europe, but also being able to talk with God and think through my future.

Looking forward to my new carefree nomadic existence, I flew off to Luxembourg on Icelandic Airlines with $400 in my pocket and a three-month Eurorail pass. I crisscrossed Europe, visiting Spain, France, Germany, Portugal and even traveling for a while in Morocco, in North Africa.

As I was traveling around, I was always open to new ideas about where I should go next. So when I was told there was a beautiful woman at L'Abri, a Christian community in the mountain village of Huemoz, Switzerland, I thought that should be my next stop. I had heard about Francis Schaeffer, the founder of L'Abri, which means "shelter", named because it was to be a community of people who were seeking some shelter from the storm of secular culture, a place where people could study and think about life, philosophy and their relationship with God.

Dr. Schaeffer and his wife Edith began this work in 1955 when they opened up their home to people who were looking for answers. Evangelicalism was a very weak voice in society at that time. Theological liberalism was very strong. The Schaeffers wanted to provide a biblical defense of Christianity that was both compassionate and credible from an intellectual viewpoint.

Some residents were non-Christians who were interested in Christianity; others were Christians questioning their faith; while others wanted to be able to answer the questions of others. And some just wanted to learn how to let Christ be Lord of their whole life, not just a part of it.

For whatever reason, thousands of people from all over the world had gone to the L'Abri Fellowship since 1955 to find answers. Dr. Schaeffer was known as a great Christian philosopher. So I took the train to Lausanne, Switzerland, and then another mountain train up through the clouds into the beautiful old world Alpine village of Huemoz. As I got off the train I could hear the sound of church bells chiming across the valley and the clanking of cow bells closer by.

Taking a deep breath of the champagne-like air, I found the main chalet at L'Abri, where it was decided whether you could stay longer or not. I looked around for the girl, but when I found this young blonde, I could tell by her body language that she wasn't too impressed with me, so I thought, *I'm not too impressed with you, either, lady.*

I decided that if I could, I would like to stay at L'Abri for a while. I knew that I fit the criteria. I was a philosophy major from a secular university. I was hurt and, as a result, was cynical about organized Christianity. I was also a bit of a rebel.

So, as I had expected, they invited me to stay. I was told, however, that I would be staying just over the mountain in French L'Abri, which was located in another village over the French border just a few miles away. I was a bit disappointed to be sent to the French one, because I thought there was more status in being at Swiss L'Abri.

When I arrived there, I discovered many different types of people staying in the chalet. One was a guy from New York who seemed to be in his thirties. I think he was a film-maker. He said he was really searching for truth and asked lots of questions. Another was a girl from Canada from a background similar to mine. There was also a guy in his twenties from Texas, and one of the discussion group leaders was an Englishman named Davey, who was your stereotypical uptight British guy who always looked as it he had an offensive smell permanently under his nostrils.

Like all L'Abri students, I spent half of each day doing chores at the chalet and the other half studying in L'Abri's library. Most of the study consisted of listening to taped lectures on various topics, with some reading. A worker in charge helped each of us with a customized course of study.

I had a very pleasant work duty. One of my jobs was to walk the Burmese mountain dog every evening in the mountains. I would go for long walks and, during this time, would have long discussions with God under a curtain of ruby stars. He was just beginning the process of restoring me in those moon-washed mountains.

Francis Schaeffer invited me to have dinner one night with him at his chalet in the Swiss L'Abri. He was a small, stocky, rather intense man, with a goatee beard, and clad in sort of leather knickerbockers trousers. He was the most humble man I had ever met. He treated everyone with respect whether they were a prominent scientist or celebrity, or just a kid off the street. L'Abri had become a sanctuary for many wounded Christians from all over the world, particularly deep thinkers and creative people who somehow felt alienated from mainstream Christianity.

Also at our meal was his wife, Edith, and a Venezuela businessman who had made a fortune in oil. As we ate I gazed out of the picture window of their chalet at the breathtaking mountain view, which was quiet, fresh and verdant. I asked him what he thought about the seminary I was considering.

"I don't think that would be a good place for you to go, David," he said, without hesitation.

"Why not?" I asked.

He said he didn't agree with some of their theological stands, but that wasn't important to me. What was, was that it gave me an excuse not to go.

My initial six-week trip was growing into something nearer six months, and I was fast running out of money. I felt my time at L'Abri was over, and so I hitch-hiked to Amsterdam to meet my friend Judy who I was told was staying at The Ark, an establishment based on two old houseboats latched together and located on the harbor behind the Central Station. These big old hulks were being used as a center for a group called Youth With A Mission.

Judy had been one of the few who had stood by me during the demise of Everybody's House. She had lived next door to it in a sorority, a student housing organization for coeds. An attractive girl with long brown hair, Judy was extremely intelligent. But she also liked to have lots of fun, so she was initially attracted to one of our parties.

During one of our exuberant snake dances Judy came to the front and actually led it for a time. Then she started coming to our Bible studies. She would sit by the door, listen intently, and then leave without talking to anybody. But one day, at a student cafe, she told me over a cup of coffee how she had invited Jesus into her life.

I didn't understand completely why she was in Amsterdam, because she had a scholarship from the University of Minnesota to study French, but I was very anxious to see her. After being away for so long, I thought it would be great to see someone from home.

It was a cold, dreary, rainy night when I arrived at the Central Station in Amsterdam. I walked along the pier, past a line of floating house boats, bobbing up and down on the cold gray water of the Ij, the river that divides the north and south sectors of Amsterdam and ultimately winds its way out to the North Sea. The Ark was at Steiger 14, which means Pier 14 in Dutch.

I crossed a wooden plank and knocked on The Ark's big, broad door. It was opened by a large, smiling young man who ushered me into what was called "The Afghan Room." There were small tables on the floor with candles and a vast array of radical looking hippies sitting cross-legged on the floor having discussions with each other. It was difficult to tell which were from the street and which were from The Ark.

I immediately liked the place because it reminded me of our ministry at the university.

I was approached by a tall man with long, blond hair who looked like Eddie Vedder on a bad day. "I'm looking for Judy Hellander," I said.

"You just missed her," he said in a thick, German accent. "She's just gone to the farm."

As I was about to ask what the farm was, he said, "But you're lucky, there's someone going there right now. You can get a ride with him."

So another Eddie Vedder look-alike drove me in his old VW Bug to the farm. It seemed to take hours to get there, although in actuality, Epe, a picturesque little hamlet, is only about sixty miles to the north of Amsterdam. The driver just stared blankly straight ahead through the rain as the windshield wipers clicked back and forth. He never uttered one word during the whole journey, his face set in a scowl.

I discovered the farm was a former leper colony on the edge of a forest. I got out of the car as dusk was falling and saw a hippie girl coming out of the kitchen wearing a peasant dress.

"Hi, do you know where Judy is?" I asked.

"She's taking a walk in the forest," the girl answered with a New Zealand accent. I started walking in the direction she had pointed.

When we saw each other on a path, Judy began running towards me and threw her arms around me and gave me an emotional hug. "David, I'm so excited to see you," she said breathlessly.

"What are you doing here?" I asked.

"I'm praying for Menbain," she responded, her eyes bright with enthusiasm.

"You're praying for where?" I responded with a puzzled look crossing my face.

"Menbain," she repeated.

"Where's that?" I asked her.

"I don't know," she smiled.

"It's so great you're here tonight, because tonight we're having the Love Feast."

As she spoke, something inside me had begun to sound an alarm.

"Judy, this place is a cult! You need to get out of here."

My warning appeared to make a big impression on her, because she looked upon me as her spiritual big brother.

"Anyway, I thought you were supposed to be in Paris studying French. You need to go back to Paris and study French."

Judy said that she thought I should meet Floyd McClung, who, she explained, headed up the farm. I had heard this man speak when I was at the university and I thought he was a cool guy. I couldn't understand why he was involved with this cult.

I was nearly out of money. When we met, Floyd, a gentle giant of a man, he told me if I did some practical work then I could stay there and eat. I felt I was strong enough to not be affected by the cult, and in the meantime I might persuade Judy to agree to go back to Paris to study French. So, at least I was helping to get her out.

My job on the farm was to carry bricks for a fireplace that was being built and also to help Floyd put some bookshelves in his office.

Before Judy left for Paris, she told me that they were going to have what she called an "outreach" in Amsterdam with a powerful English evangelist named John Goodfellow. I thought it would be a pleasant change to get into the city for a while, so I agreed to go along.

About forty of us met behind the Central Station in the Afghan Room, on The Ark while John Goodfellow explained what the strategy would be.

"We'll go to the main square in the city, form a half circle, sing a few songs and those that wish to talk about what God has done for them can, and some of us will then preach," he said in a thick Nottingham accent.

John Goodfellow, who was resplendent with long hair and bell-bottom blue jeans, seemed authentic to me.

We marched off to Dam Square and, as we stood in a half circle, I started to get an overwhelming feeling that I should preach. The impression was so powerful that I felt as if my heart was going to jump out of my body.

Finally, I couldn't stand it anymore and so I walked over to McClung and I said, "Floyd, I'd like to say something."

To my astonishment, he said, "No, David. You can't."

My face clouded with disbelief. This really devastated me and so I left the group and I went over to a bench on the square and sat down. After the meeting was over, the group broke up to talk to people on the square. Not knowing that I was with them, somebody came up to me and asked me if I wanted to know God.

"No," I snapped sullenly.

And so the person walked away.

We stayed on The Ark for a few days. Later on that week, Judy and I met somebody on the street and they seemed to be very close to giving their heart to Jesus. So we decided to spend the night in prayer for this guy. But during that night, I found myself also praying about my future.

As we sat on the edge of a pier on that freezing cold night, I cried out to God, asking him what he wanted me to do with my life. The next day, Judy and I were back in Dam Square; and someone came up to me and said, "I want to give this to you. Is that OK?"

"Sure," I said, thinking it was an advertisement for a store.

It turned out to be one hundred guilders, or the equivalent of 60 US dollars. I had been out of money for quite some time, so this was really great; Judy and I had a Chinese dinner.

That same day, back at The Ark, Floyd came up to me and said, "David, I think you should really come back here and work with us."

I liked Floyd and I appreciated him asking me, but I knew that it couldn't be of God because this was a cult. I flew back to America but I could not get what Floyd had said out of my mind. So I prayed, "God if that was really you, have Floyd write me a personal letter this week inviting me to come."

The very next day I went to my mail box and there was a hand-written letter from Floyd. I tore it open. "Remember our conversation in Amsterdam?" it read. "I think you need to come."

I knew that this wasn't a coincidence and that, if I didn't go, I'd be like Jonah. I didn't know what was going to swallow me in Minnesota, but I wasn't going to take any chances.

So I phoned Floyd. "Floyd," I said over the trans-Atlantic line, "I don't have any money, or support."

"Don't worry; just come and we'll trust God to provide the money."

I worked for six months as a carpenter in Minneapolis, sold everything I owned, and prepared to return to Europe. I had no doubt in my mind that God was asking me to do this. I knew that YWAM was certainly not a cult, in fact, it was where God wanted me to be so that he could mold me into the kind of person that he could use.

5
THE YUGOSLAV BRIGADE

IT WAS A COLD, DARK, dismal January day on the farm in Holland, later called Heidebeek, and I was wondering what I was doing sitting in that room.

"I had a dream and God told me that I was going to be sent to the nations," said one young English girl, her face radiant and alive with enthusiasm. "And so when I heard about this school, there was a real confirmation in my spirit." With that she broke into tears and sat down.

I looked at the floor, bit down on my lip and tried not to laugh. I then let my gaze stray about the room in a manner calculated to suggest to the assembled group that I was bored and was paying little attention to the proceedings.

A young Dutch man volunteered to be next. "Hello, my name is Rinus," he said, pausing to give effect to his words. I thought to myself, *Rinus! You've got to be joking. What kind of name is that?*

He continued, as I yawned loudly, "I grew up in the Dutch Reformed Church and I'm so grateful that I can be here in this school because of all the things that I'm going to be able to learn." A ripple of polite applause broke out from around the room and he acknowledged the response.

I thought that I had better break my silence and get my speech over with. I raised my hand and then rose to my feet. "I don't know why I'm here and I don't want to be here," I said petulantly. With my brief speech over, I sat down heavily. My words had had a paralyzing effect. No one applauded, and an embarrassed silence swept over the room. I had given a convincing impression of indifference. One of the DTS leaders glared at me, his mouth tight and grim.

I guess I was an impossible student. The leaders of the school were always trying to figure out ways to manage me. On Monday mornings we were supposed to gather for intercessory prayer for different countries. My group met in a little bungalow that was heated by a small gas burner.

The meeting started at 8:30 a.m. and I was usually still sleepy around that time. I also couldn't get used to the idea of praying for some place that I'd never been to. So I would sit in a big, soft chair by the gas burner, and Moses, a little sheep dog, would jump into my lap, and we would both go to sleep, closing our lazy-lidded eyes.

Everybody had to take turns doing dishes in the school, and they even had dish squad leaders. It would really irritate me that I was never asked to be one. I thought, *I can't believe these people. Can't I even be a lousy dish squad leader? Don't they know that back in America I once led a whole ministry?*

But still, I took comfort in the knowledge that my big day was coming. There was going to be an evangelistic street meeting in Amsterdam and this would be my opportunity to show them that I was a great preacher. I had long discussions with John Goodfellow, who was one of the leaders of the school, on how great it was going to be when we went into the city. He had been assigned by the other leaders to watch me, so that I wouldn't be too much of a bad influence on the other students.

The day before we were to go into the city, one of the female leaders, whom I didn't like very much, came into the bungalow. She overheard me talking to John about the upcoming meeting.

"You're not going anywhere," she said with a grin as hard as a car grille. "You're on dish duty." I felt my strength drain away. I was speechless, I stormed out of the bungalow into the nearby dark, cold woods.

Enraged at this woman and this school that I found myself involved with, I stumbled in a daze into a steel-gray curtain of rain. As I was walking along a path, I don't know how it happened, but I suddenly found myself lying face down, sobbing in the freezing mud in a field. Rain continued to soak into me from an unrelenting sky.

"OK, God, I give up," I cried, feeling a sudden stab of remorse. "I just want to get to know you better. I don't care what I do anymore. If you want me to stay and do the dishes, then I'll do them." By now, my trembling voice was almost inaudible.

Covered in mud, I rose to my feet, feeling some-how purged of my anger. This extraordinary incident on that frigid night was the beginning of a major breakthrough in my life. After that, I would go for long walks into the woods with Moses. Often I would go in the middle of the night, for up to five hours at a time, just to spend this time communing with God. I went at night because it was eerie and that made me concentrate better. Often I would be out in the freezing cold rain, but that somehow didn't seem to matter.

To an outsider, I was not somebody God could use for his service. And many of the leaders of the mission had come to that same conclusion. But God doesn't call people because of anything good in themselves. He calls sinful, struggling people into his service, and I certainly qualified under that criterion.

Ed Harrington came from an extremely rigid background in America and had been involved in drugs. Later he cried out to God when he thought he was dying from a drug overdose. After the DTS, Ed and I headed out to Yugoslavia after hearing about a terrible earthquake in Ulcinj, near the Albanian border.

We traveled by train to the province of Montenegro and went to the office of the Yugoslavian National Guard in the earthquake. "We are from America and we heard about the earthquake and we would like to volunteer to be a part of your National Guard," I said.

The officer looked at us with astonishment. "Don't be ridiculous," he said. "You're Americans. That's impossible. Please go away."

Undeterred, Ed decided that we were going too quickly and that we needed to fast and pray for a couple of days and then ask again. I hate fasting and was glad when Ed said we could stop and that we should try again with the authorities. As we finished our fast, a family living in a tent because their home had been destroyed by the earthquake, asked us into their tent, so we accepted their invitation.

We were each handed a glass of something by this tough Yugoslavian guy. We thought we had better take some or they would be offended. As I drank, my whole body felt a rush. It was a powerful alcoholic drink possessing a kick like a mule.

Again, we went back to the government office and asked if we could volunteer. To our surprise, the very same man who appeared to be still wearing the same smelly shirt, said we could. The next thing we knew, we were issued green army uniforms with a Yugoslavian patch on the front. We were now enrolled in the Yugoslavian Communist brigade.

We lived in a camp with about 200 other men and a few dozen women. At 5 a.m. we were awakened by a Yugoslavian style reveille, and then we all did exercises in a field. Then they would raise the Yugoslavian flag and everybody would proudly sing the Yugoslavian national anthem.

We would set off each morning in big open trucks to work on roads or houses damaged by the earthquake. The camp had a curfew and you needed a pass to leave and return. At first we were followed everywhere by the local soldiers. They must have thought we were American spies, but after a while the situation changed for us. The Commandant became a close friend and he would invite me into his tent and ask questions about the Bible and God. Soon we could come and go as we pleased and God gave us real favor in the camp. All the men there were hard drinkers and smokers. They would start drinking hard liquor at five o'clock in the morning and they smoked unfiltered cigarettes all day long.

Montenegro is known for its big, strong, hospitable people. They are hard-drinking, rough, but friendly. We thought we'd never be able to share the gospel with all the people in the camp. One day Ed got the idea of buying a bunch of cigarettes and cutting up long note paper on which to write the text of John 3:16,17. He carefully inscribed on each the following in Croatian:

For God so loved the world that he gave his one and only Son, that whoever believes in him shall not perish but have eternal life. For God did not send his Son into the world to condemn the world, but to save the world through him.

We gave a little gift of a cigarette with a gospel message note attached to everyone in the camp.

Often at night we would have group discussions in a big tent about Jesus. Somebody in the camp would translate or I would look up the verse in my English Bible and point to the same in the Yugoslavian Bible and have someone read it.

The greatest honor they could bestow on anyone in the camp was to have them lower the flag at the end of the day. I'll never forget the moment they asked me to lower the flag and I proudly went through the ritual, while people stood and sang the national anthem, tears stinging their eyes.

While we were there, a Yugoslavian TV crew came and interviewed us. They asked me why we were there. I told them it was because Jesus loved Yugoslavia. I could tell by their reaction that they thought that Jesus was a guy in the States. Local newspapers also wrote up the story of our coming.

One day we were working on repairing a damaged road. Ed asked the Commandant what the road was used for. He explained that it was the road to the local nudist colony for tourists. So here we were, missionaries fixing a road to a nudist colony! We asked if we could do some other work, and, remarkably, he agreed.

One afternoon, I was sitting in an outdoor cafe by the Adriatic Sea talking to a guy about Jesus. I explained to him that there was a serious decision before him concerning giving his life over to God. Suddenly, there was an earthquake and everyone was screaming. You could see the beach move back and forth in one piece. It was an awesome sight. The little thatched cafe became a blur as we literally hung on to our chairs. It was exciting in a way and I figured we weren't in any danger unless the ground opened up. When the quake stopped, I looked at the man calmly and said, "In the Bible it says that in the end times there will be earthquakes." He listened more carefully after that!

Early one morning, while we were repairing a damaged house, I walked round the corner of the building and stumbled on some broken glass. My right leg was cut nearly to the bone. Ed quickly took off his shirt and used it as a tourniquet so that I wouldn't bleed to death. He managed to get a taxi that took me to the hospital. We were fortunate to survive the taxi ride as the driver careened around the mountainous curves. We slid round one corner on two wheels. The hospital was just a group of tents with white material on the inside to give an appearance of cleanliness. There were long lines of sick and wounded people waiting to see the doctor. Because I was a foreigner, they put me at the front of the line and I got in immediately. The doctor stitched up my leg and Ed took me to one of the tents. The nurses sat outside the tents and smoked cigarettes, hardly paying any attention at all to the patients.

Every morning breakfast consisted of tea with lots of sugar in it, and goat cheese on white bread. There was no running water except for a pipe sticking out of the ground outside the tent. Lying next to me was a very sick old man; I gave a Yugoslavian Bible to him. The only way I could communicate with the nurses was to speak my broken French to the dying man next to me, and he would talk to them in Croatian.

It wasn't surprising that in these conditions, I soon developed a bad case of diarrhea. The only toilets were outside the tents, some fifty yards away.

They were actually nothing more than holes in the ground. The idea was that you would squat above the hole. Because of my wound, I could only stand on one leg. It was quite a challenge to squat on one leg.

The conditions in the hospital were so bad that we decided it would be better for me to try and recover elsewhere, so after three days I left.

The Communist brigade had now completed its task, so Ed and I headed for the Yugoslav capital in Belgrade. We found an open field and decided to live there for a while so that my leg could get better. The problem was that we had no tent, only sleeping bags. Every time it rained we would have to take cover under a tree—and it always seemed to rain at night. During that month, we ate only raw vegetables, raw eggs and bread. To eat the eggs, we would take a small rock and chip a hole on both sides of the egg, and then suck out the contents. It wasn't bad once you got used to it. For some reason, it was taking a long time for my leg to heal. I was frustrated because we still had some Bibles we wanted to give to people who had been in the nearby camp, but who had now returned to their towns and villages.

I wanted to deliver the Bibles even though my leg wasn't better, so we decided to split up to deliver them faster. I was supposed to hitchhike to a particular village which I did, but that night, lying on a bench, shivering because of the cold, my leg hurting, I felt that this was becoming a real test of my faith.

Finally, I cried out, "OK God, if you want me to be cold and limp around delivering these Bibles, I will."

The next morning my leg improved and I could walk normally by the end of the day. I thought I had just passed a major test in my relationship with the Lord. And I was right. God had wanted to see if I would be willing to do literally anything that he asked of me, and I was!

It was an important lesson for the future.

THE 6COFFIN

ON RETURNING FROM YUGOSLAVIA, I moved to The Cleft located in the center of Amsterdam as a part of John Goodfellow's team. This place, named after the source of fresh water that Moses found in the desert when he struck the rock with his staff, was in the very heart of the infamous red light district. As you went out of the door, on the right was The Church of Satan. This "church" had established itself there and was in control of many of the live sex shows and prostitutes in the neighborhood. On the left was a pornographic cinema. The whole block was filled with houses of prostitution.

Heroin-prostitutes stood on the bridges, and the upper class prostitutes sat behind windows, backlit by red fluorescent lights, reclining on couches, dressed in their nightgowns, so that the tourists going by could pick out the girls they wanted.

One day, as I was walking through the city, I got a strong impression that I needed to go up to my room and pray. I didn't often get this kind of thought, so I knew I had better do it! I knelt by my bed, not knowing what I should be praying about. Suddenly I had an overwhelming feeling that I should be willing to be single for the rest of my life if that was what God wanted. I was now twenty-five years old and wasn't really thinking about marriage.

"God," I prayed, "if you want me to be single for the rest of my life, I'm willing to be so."

I left my room and headed back out onto the street and forgot about the incident. The next day, I was getting ready for what we called our Summer Outreach program. College students from all over the world were joining us for a few weeks of intensive evangelism. Someone from the team said, "Hey, David, there's this really good-looking blonde German girl that has just arrived. You should meet her."

I felt it was my duty to make sure she was OK. As we were preparing to go to the main part of the city, a friend told me in a conspiratorial tone, "There she is, up ahead." The girl looked good to me from the back, so I picked up my pace to overtake her and see what she looked like from the front. But before I got in front of her one of the girls got my attention and said, "David, I want you to meet somebody."

She introduced me to the German girl. "I'd like you to meet Jodi Smith," she said. I was to discover that Jodi was not German at all, but American. Not only that, but she was from my home town of Minneapolis.

"Are you David Pierce?" she asked.

"Yes, I am." Hoping that was the right answer, because at this point I had just fallen wildly in love with her.

"I know you," she said.

"You do?"

"We went to the same church together in Brooklyn Center."

"We did?"

It turned out that we didn't really know each other because she sat in the front of the church and I was always at the back. But not only was she from my church, but her father was at my father's wedding.

I thought of what I had prayed the night before and I felt strangely that, because I had showed God that I was willing to be single, he was now going to give me a wife.

I was having coffee with one of my friends, Marwin, the next day and I told her that I had met the girl that I was going to marry. She laughed at me and told me that I was crazy.

From then on, Jodi and I were almost inseparable, except when I was in my coffin! I'll explain that. One of the problems that we faced in Amsterdam, was that 97% of the people never attended church. And of the 3% that did, hardly any were young people.

If I told someone in Amsterdam that I was a Christian, immediately there was a wall between me and that person.

"Oh, yeah," they would say. "I know what a Christian is. Aren't they killing each other in Belfast?" Oh, "A Christian, isn't that a political ideology? Aren't Christians pro-nuclear weapons?" Or maybe they thought of the big beautiful church that I could see from where I lived. This old cathedral was visited by tourists from all over the world. The church bell was rung by a homosexual. The church, which was often closed, was completely surrounded by houses of prostitution that were always open.

So the idea most people in that city had of Christianity was that of a dead, empty tradition. Jesus was totally irrelevant to their lives. But I knew him to be the most exciting and relevant person there is.

Jesus always tried to communicate in the symbols of the people he was trying to reach out to. When he talked to farmers he talked about wineskins and vineyards; when he talked to fishermen he said, "I want to make you fishers of men." When he talked to shepherds he said, "I am the good shepherd who cares for the flock."

But I was aware that if I went up to someone in Amsterdam and said that Jesus was the Good Shepherd, they wouldn't have the slightest idea what I was talking about because there aren't a lot of sheep running around Amsterdam. So I prayed, asking God what symbol I could use to get people's attention.

The problem we faced in the city was that so many of the people thought they had already heard the message about Jesus, but really they never had. The Jesus they rejected was one whom I would also reject. I believed that if they really knew who Jesus was, they would want to have a relationship with him.

So the challenge was how am I going to get them to listen. One day an idea came to me. It was the unusual that would capture their imaginations. So I built a big, black coffin. Then, with a team of about thirty, we would have a funeral procession through the city. Each time before we started, we would ask God to give us his "broken heart" for the city. We wanted to know how he felt about the sex shops that specialized in child pornography, about the godlessness in the universities and the thousands of drug addicts that were dying without hope throughout Amsterdam.

The "pall bearers" would carry the coffin, two at the front and two on the back. We would go through the red light district, past the Hell's Angels bar and the outdoor cafes. The people sitting there crossed themselves, because they weren't sure if somebody was in the coffin or not. Someone *was* in the coffin—me! And I was dressed in black with black make-up around my eyes.

Before we got to the square, John Goodfellow was already there with his outreach team. They stood in a half circle singing nice Christian songs with an acoustic guitar and tambourines. Then we would arrive, led by lit torches. Our group would set the coffin right in the middle of John Goodfellow and his team. Those with the torches would surround the coffin, so you would have a ring of fire and smoke. (I got the idea from a Frankenstein movie!)

People would run towards the square to see what was happening. Now when you're in a coffin and you're not dead, time goes by very slowly. The first time I did it, I wanted to jump out as quickly as possible. So I had to think of a way to make myself stay in the coffin for a while. I would start to count down: "Ten, nine, eight, seven...four, three, two, one, zero." Then I would jump out of the coffin and begin screaming at the top of my lungs.

"This city killed me with its lies," I would shout. "You told me that I would find wisdom in your universities. But you're not wise. You can't even solve your own problems. You told me I'd find freedom in your sex shops, but you didn't make me free. You just gave me a dirty mind.

"You told me I'd find happiness in your drugs, but they didn't make me happy. They just destroyed my body. Nobody in this city cares. Nobody in this city loves. And we're all dead!"

I would then fall over on top of the coffin.

John Goodfellow would then get up on a table and say, "Hey, you there, it's true, the ways of men lead to death. Let me tell you about a way that leads to life."

The crowd loved it. They thought, *Isn't this great? The dumb Christian is trying to argue with the crazy guy.* They didn't know we were together.

"Why should I listen to you," I would mock. "Everyone's told me their better ideas. And look where it's got me."

John replied, "I'm not here to tell you about my better ideas. I'm here to tell you the truth about God that you can read for yourself in the Bible."

"The Bible—that's a bunch of religious garbage!" I would retort.

"Well, let me ask you a question," John responded. "Have you ever read the Bible?"

"Why should I?"

"Because, in the Bible you can find out who you are, who God is and your purpose for living."

The crowd that was watching did not know that we were together so they would hang on to every word we were saying. And for the first time many of them heard the message of who Jesus truly is. Then I would address the crowd.

"Amsterdam, it's true," I would say. "I was dead, but Jesus made me alive again. If you knew the person I was and know the kind of person I am now, you would know that this is true. Why don't you, in a city that is known for freedom, become really free!

"If Jesus can give me a new life, he can give it to you, too."

Then I would invite the people to kneel with me on the cobblestones and give their lives to Jesus. Through this drama many people found Christ.

John Goodfellow was becoming more than a little concerned about my relationship with Jodi, because it was against the rules for staff members to date girls on the outreach team. So, to keep us apart, he had Jodi involved in an outreach to a campsite nearby and he had me go out to a bridge near where I lived in the red light district, with five women and one quiet guy.

To get to the bridge, we had to pass by the pornographic cinema, several sex shops, then through a narrow alley with half-dressed prostitutes sitting in the windows on both sides. The bridge looked out over an area where all the live sex theaters were located.

Every evening it was the same thing: we would sing three or four songs that I hated, led by one girl who played guitar and another who had a tambourine. We would sing songs like, "This is the day, this is the day, that the Lord has made..." And while we sang it rained....

As I stood there, I thought, *No wonder no one wants to be a Christian.* And I felt really embarrassed for God. I thought to myself, *What am I going to do? God can't want me to stand on this bridge with these five women and one quiet guy and sing these stupid little songs.*

What made it even worse was that a woman would preach. I not only resented being led in worship by her, but I thought I could preach way better than she could. So I came up with a strategy; I decided to stand off to the side and act like I wasn't with the group. Wearing my black leather jacket, I would just act cool and talk to people as they walked by. This is what I would do, night after night.

It was another evening and we were again mixing with the tourists, the prostitutes and drug addicts. I was prepared to do what I did on all the other nights. But then suddenly I felt a strong conviction from God.

"You're not concerned about my reputation; you're concerned about *your* reputation," I felt God was saying to me. "You're not willing to be foolish for me."

"Do you mean that you want me to stand on this bridge and sing these stupid songs with these five women and this quiet guy?" I asked. "Is this *really* what you want me to do?"

"Yes," I felt God say to my heart. "That's really what I want you to do."

This made me very angry. And I thought, "OK, if you want me to sing, I'll sing." So I sang so loud that my voice echoed off the surrounding buildings. And it sounded like I was singing lead vocals and everyone else was singing backup. People would get angry and throw things out of the windows at us.

But that made me sing more loudly. I don't remember anyone finding God on that bridge, but maybe that wasn't God's prime intention just then. What did happen was that something of pride was broken within me, and my relationship with God was stronger than it had ever been before.

With the summer nearly over, we went back to the farm to get out of the city. Jodi and I were walking in a beautiful heather field and I knew it was now or never; I had to make my move. As we sat down on a rustic bench by a path, I cleared my throat and said as calmly as I could, "It's beautiful here, isn't it?" But I wasn't calm at all. My heart was pounding. Was I going to chicken out? *No,* I thought, *I can do it. I jump out of coffins, don't I?*

I looked her straight in the eyes and said, "Jodi, will you marry me?"

She hesitated. "Stay here, I'm going to go for a walk," she said.

Time went into slow-motion. It seemed like hours, but actually she was away for only five minutes.

"Sure," she replied, her face breaking into a smile so powerful it filled out her flushed cheeks. "We had better go and call my parents and tell them the news."

When my parents heard that I was engaged to a good Christian hometown girl, they were thrilled. Jodi's side of the family, however, wasn't so thrilled. We had only known each other for a few weeks before we got engaged and Jodi had been going with another fine young man before she met me.

So in September 1979 we returned to Minnesota to prepare for a December 29th wedding. Because things were a little tense with Jodi's side of the family, I left most of the planning to Jodi and her mother. I figured if I could just get through the ceremony without offending anyone, that would be a major accomplishment.

All went well on the big day. It was foggy and the roads were sheet ice, but fortunately there were no major problems and I don't think I offended anyone too badly.

But Jodi's side of the family were definitely not impressed with me. She was anxious to show them that the guy she had just married was not really a flake. In the meantime, we had met with Scott and some of my friends in Minneapolis and told them what a wonderful tool the coffin was in telling people about Jesus.

"It's the only way to reach people," I enthused, as I told glorious coffin stories.

"We *must* build a coffin," Scott said. "We *must* do the coffin in Minneapolis!"

Everyone agreed. And so, in Scott's basement, we worked on a beautiful black coffin. Jodi thought that this would give her family an opportunity to see something of my ministry. She hoped that when they saw the coffin routine, they would like me.

So she told two of her brothers, Lance and Steve, "David is going to do his coffin drama in Minneapolis. You have to come and see it. It's a powerful tool that God uses."

They agreed. On the fateful night, Scott, my friends and the coffin were waiting at the end of the famous downtown one mile long, tree-lined Nicollet Mall, in front of the 57-story IDS Building, perhaps the most famous in the city. Jodi's two brothers, Lance and Steve were there. I had talked my other brother-in-law, Tim Herzog, into playing the part that John Goodfellow usually played and we had rehearsed hard for the big moment.

After praying, I climbed into my coffin and we started the march down the Nicollet Mall towards the IDS Building. The "pall bearers" passed the great variety of shops and restaurants, passed the many fountains, a weather station and a clock that was also a moving sculpture. As the coffin approached the skyscraper, people from the stores saw the coffin being carried to the middle of the square, and a few came out to see what was happening.

When it was laid on the floor, I began to count down as more curious people gathered around the coffin: "Ten, nine, eight, seven . . . four, three, two, one, zero!" I jumped out of the coffin and I started screaming at the top of my lungs.

And everybody ran away.

I found myself standing alone on top of the coffin looking at my wife and her two brothers and my other brother-in-law, Tim. People were hiding in the stores and I felt completely humiliated as I picked up my coffin and went home.

It was quite some time before Jodi's brothers would talk to me after that. But I did learn an important lesson. It was that what God had taught me in Amsterdam was good, but the way I had tried to apply it in Minneapolis wasn't. It wasn't good enough for me to understand spiritual principles alone. I also needed to understand the culture that I was trying to reach. I must apply the principles effectively and communicate the gospel in a way that people can understand.

One of the great things that happened after I married Jodi was that a church finally agreed to support us financially. We began to receive $150 a month support from Faith Baptist Fellowship in Sioux Falls, South Dakota. But we needed to find a lot more money somewhere if we were to be able to buy plane tickets back to Europe.

We decided to sell all our wedding gifts to do that, but we still didn't have quite enough money. Jodi had received a beautiful set of china from her family at the wedding, and one day she came to me and said she thought she should sell the china.

"Are you sure?" I asked.

"God can always give me dishes again if I need dishes," she said.

It did the trick, and we made our way back to Amsterdam for our new life together.

7 LIVING WITH LOST SHEEP

THE SOUNDS OF BREAKING GLASS brought me to the window of our little apartment on the edge of the red light district. Living where we did, we didn't need a TV, because you could look out of the window and see robbing, mugging and all kinds of excitement taking place in the street below.

I focused on the mayhem of a full-blown riot. A group of English soccer fans were in town and had decided they wanted to fight with the drug dealers. So up and down the street about eighty people ran, armed with bricks, bottles and clubs. The whooping English soccer fans chased the drug dealers from the street. But their victory was short-lived. The drug dealers began frantically digging up the cobblestones and then, armed with their new ammunition, they chased the English fans back again.

Screams and the sounds of breaking glass reverberated through the nearby buildings as this battle raged.

Suddenly a solitary police car screeched into the parking lot across from our building and an officer jumped out of the car and ran into the angry mob with a rubber truncheon. What was surprising was what the protagonists did. I knew they could have eaten this guy for lunch but instead they dropped their bottles, bricks, cobblestones and clubs, and all ran together down a nearby alleyway with the lone officer with the rubber stick in hot pursuit.

Suddenly, he realized what he was doing, obviously became frightened and quickly retreated to the relative safety of his police car. But for a while at least, for a few crazy moments, the policeman believed in what he represented. He was convinced that the power and the authority of the law was greater than the power and the authority of the mob.

As I witnessed this, I came to see that God was asking Jodi and myself to be like the policeman before he got scared. Did we believe in whom we represented? Would we be willing to live among the lost sheep and face the dangerous consequences?

After returning to Holland and completing another training school for Youth With A Mission staff, Jodi and I began to run a coffee house on the edge of the red light district. The coffee house was part of a bigger building called the Samaritan's Inn, which was formerly a rundown budget hotel. It was a dirty and derelict rabbit-warren of a building and YWAM staff were in the process of restoring it.

We held daily Bible studies for new Christians in "Sam's Inn" and also a nightly outreach into the red light district. We used the coffee house for friendship evangelism which was gentle, low-key and long-term. We also held Bible studies for new Christians.

At that time we lived upstairs in a room the size of a large closet. It was small and functional, with almost an army barracks flavor. We only had a blanket for a door. We slept on the floor in two sleeping bags; Jodi had to dust plaster that had fallen from the ceiling during the previous night off the sleeping bags every morning.

There was only one toilet, which we were obliged to share with sixty people. The building had no hot water and, because we were trying to live on

$150 a month support, the only form of entertainment we could afford was going for a walk around the crowded streets. Sometimes, if we were really fortunate, we would be able to get a cup of coffee in a sidewalk cafe along the way.

One day, as we were returning to the Samaritan's Inn, Akie, a Pakistani man, came running towards us. He was someone that Jodi and I had led to Christ and who was attending our weekly Bible study.

"The building's on fire," he shouted in a terrified voice. We ran to the Inn and saw smoke pouring out of one of the windows. After further investigation, we discovered that the fire was located in just one place—our room.

Apparently, a welder in the room up above had accidentally sent some sparks through the ceiling into our room and started the fire. The sparks landed on top of Jodi's clothes and burned them all up, including some nice nightgowns she had received at our wedding. As I thought about how I could comfort her, she surprised me with her reaction.

"It's no big deal," she said softly. "Everything will be fine. It's only clothes that have gone."

It was at that moment that I realized that I was married to a combination of Claudia Schiffer and Mother Teresa!

Soon after that we moved around the corner to the Zeedyke. At that time the area was known throughout Holland as a most dangerous place to live. It was on the edge of the red light district and home to most of the drug trading in Amsterdam.

In Amsterdam, there is an extreme housing shortage. To find any place to live is extremely difficult. We had one room to live in. It was formerly used by a prostitute. The bed was gigantic, with mirrors everywhere. You had to unlock four doors to enter our room. Before we could go into the building, we often had to wait for someone to stop vomiting or urinating by our door.

Next to our room was a bath. One night, while I was taking a bath, I heard Jodi screaming. I had just soaked my hair, so my face was covered with shampoo. I thought that maybe somebody had broken in and so I jerked open the door and ran into the room stark naked, with my face covered in soap.

What had happened was that Jodi had opened the door to her closet and discovered a mouse resting comfortably on her nightgown. It wasn't that she hadn't seen a mouse before. The room was infested with them. Jodi would always knock on the door and shout, "We're coming in, mice," so they would run and hide.

This mouse, however, was the final straw and, to make things worse, Jodi was one month pregnant with our first child.

To add to her misery was the fact that, below our apartment, was an Indonesian restaurant, and the smells wafting up from it made her sick.

I knew we had to find a better place to live. I was aware this would be difficult—there was often a five-to-ten year waiting list for decent apartments in the inner city—and in fact over the next two-and-a-half years we moved ten times before we found a permanent place to live. We would often stay in one place for only a few weeks, while the owners were away on a trip.

Once, after our son Aaron was born, we actually found ourselves with nowhere to live. I put all our belongings in an old VW van. I'll never forget the feeling of desperation at having my wife, our new baby and all our worldly possessions in this old, broken-down van. As I drove around in a daze, we stopped at a red light. Rain that had been trapped up on the roof, swooped down on us through an open window. Fortunately, Jodi managed to move the baby before he got soaked.

Never once, during these difficult times, did Jodi suggest we go back home to America. Finally, we were able to find a permanent place to live in the inner city—a tiny, three-bedroom apartment just outside the red light district, down the street from a hashish bar. We moved in during 1983, and lived there for thirteen years before moving to New Zealand.

Paul Filler was one of the leaders at the farm, now called Heidebeek. He wanted to put together a drama team to preach the gospel. The drama he wanted to use was called *Toymaker and Son,* a musical parable about creation, the fall of man and salvation through Jesus, mixing drama and dance. The fifty-minute production had little narration and no dialogue, although its message soon became clear.

I thought it was a good idea, but I was glad that "God didn't call me to do that sort of thing."

I was willing to preach and sing on the bridge in the red light district with those five women and that quiet guy, but I was glad that God didn't want me to do little dances. So when Paul asked for volunteers, I knew that it wasn't for me.

Jodi got involved in a part, but we both knew it was only temporary. Unfortunately, they couldn't fill all of the roles and I was asked if I would be willing to play a part until they got somebody else.

I felt the same struggle I had experienced on the bridge.

"OK, God," I finally conceded. "If you want me to do little dances for you, I will."

I not only took a temporary part, but eventually found myself leading a drama team during the next two years. We toured throughout Europe and America and thousands of people found Christ through *Toymaker and Son*.

In April 1981 we performed our drama in the St. Sintagma Square in Athens, Greece. As some 4,000 people gathered to witness our performance of the gospel message, I was aware that here we were in the country that was Europe's first Christian outpost over 1,900 years before.

After we had finished our performance, I felt I should preach. I was aware of the dangers—it was illegal to proselytize—so, standing not far from Mars Hill where the Apostle Paul once shared the claims of Jesus Christ, I felt honored to be able to tell the Greek people the truth about the Good News.

Costas Macris, the founder of the Hellenic Gospel Mission, was my interpreter. He said it was the largest evangelistic gathering in recent history in Greece. I invited those who were ready to give their lives to Jesus to come forward.

This was the first time I had given a public altar call, and hundreds of people responded. Many of these people are involved in churches in Athens today.

Timo and Helen, the Greek couple who were organizing our performances in Athens, asked us to go with them to meet one of the wealthiest people in Greece. We arrived at a white mansion and, as we talked to our female host, we were waited on by her Egyptian servants. She invited us to perform at a private Greek amphitheater before the Prime Minister, other leading officials and prominent people in the country.

We gladly accepted. The next week, we were driven into a private estate, with villas perched on a cliff overlooking the Mediterranean. In the center was a miniature Greek amphitheater. After our performance, I was able to speak to the Prime Minister and all the other government officials there, telling them about God's love for them.

After our command performance for the Greek elite, the cast was invited to one of the villas for a party. And, as Jodi and I took a walk in one of the magnificent gardens behind one of the villas and looked at the incredible beauty laid out before us, it occurred to me why God was giving us these kinds of opportunities. It was because I had been willing to sing on that bridge in the red light district with the five women and that one quiet guy.

If I had said no to God there, it would have stopped him from being able to do what he wanted with my life.

8 THE CHRUNKS

IT WAS AN UNUSUALLY BRIGHT MORNING FOR AMSTERDAM. Dark clouds often blanketed the city, but today the sun was already high in the sky, making everything look beautiful. My spirits were also high as I made my way, at about 8:30 a.m., to a nearby Hell's Angels bar with an unrepeatably obscene name, to read my Bible. It had become my habit to go there every morning to order a cup of coffee and read.

This particular morning I entered the gloomy establishment, took my place at the bar and ordered my usual. Then, with the sound of Mick Jagger and the Rolling Stones singing "Under My Thumb" thundering out of the PA system, I opened my Bible. I had come to realize that I needed to live out my faith in the local community—and this was quite a community!

I was sitting between two burly bikers who were deeply engrossed in their motorcycle magazines. I saw, out of the corner of my eye, a picture of a shiny Harley Davidson motor cycle in one of the magazines. I decided to try to start a conversation with the reader.

"Wow, that's a cool looking bike," I said, hoping he would respond as warmly as I had spoken.

I guess I should have known that I was expecting too much at that time in the morning. He did not welcome my attempt at friendship and called me a few obscene names and told me if I didn't mind my own business, he would kill me.

Feeling somewhat frustrated, I finished my Bible study and headed back to our apartment to see Jodi and our son, Aaron.

It began to dawn on me that in Amsterdam we were reaching a lot of tourists and street people, but not the ordinary Dutch young people—those who could influence society: the trend-setters like those in the universities at one end of the spectrum, and the kids who were still in the counter-cultures at the other. I was convinced Jesus was totally relevant to their lives, and I was troubled by the fact that we weren't reaching them. I needed to know the answer to this problem.

So for the next few months I studied with great intensity what the Bible says about "lost sheep." Maybe I would discover the reason why we weren't gathering them up. The study became fascinating to me and provided many answers which were to unlock our work of sharing Christ with the lost sheep, not only in Amsterdam but also later in some of the remotest parts of the world.

"Why don't you share with some of the other staff what you have discovered?" asked John Goodfellow one day.

I stood before a group of YWAM staff in Amsterdam and told them: "After working on the streets of Amsterdam for nearly five years, I have come to see that these Dutch young people are almost completely unreached with the gospel. Our past evangelistic efforts of drama and preaching in public places have not reached them."

I explained that, on reading about the Parable of the Lost Sheep, I had become inspired by Christ's example.

Luke 15 demonstrates the strategy:

Now the tax collectors and sinners were all gathering around to hear him. But the Pharisees and the teachers of the law muttered, "This man welcomes sinners and eats with them."

Then Jesus told them this parable: "Suppose one of you has a hundred sheep and loses one of them. Does he not leave the ninety-nine in the open country and go after the sheep until he finds it? And when he finds it, he joyfully puts it on his shoulders and goes home. Then he calls his friends and neighbors together and says, 'Rejoice with me; I have found my lost sheep.'

"I tell you that in the same way there will be more rejoicing in heaven over one sinner who repents than over ninety-nine righteous persons who do not need to repent."

"The shepherd in this story had one-hundred sheep and one kept running away," I told them. "What was this lost sheep like? This was probably a very bothersome sheep! If sheep bit people, this one would. He probably didn't dress like the other sheep. It probably had a bad influence on the weaker sheep. It didn't wear his hair like the other sheep and he probably listened to strange sheep music.

Now, if I'm the shepherd, what do I do? Well, the only logical thing to do is to let him go. After all, I reason to myself, I've got ninety-nine good, respectable sheep that need me. The lost sheep is always in trouble. He's not teachable, and besides one out of a hundred isn't bad.

"So what does the normal shepherd do? He says, 'OK, I'll look. Maybe during my lunch break. After all, I've got ninety nine respectable sheep, and, if I leave them too long, they will be in danger. Somebody might steal them!'

"But what does the *good* shepherd do? He looks for the lost sheep until he finds him! A week, a month, a year—however long it takes. There is no time limit! It is very important to understand a vital principle about lost sheep. *Lost sheep are lost!*

"We often don't take that into consideration when we try to reach them. Instead, we hold Lost Sheep Rallies. We advertise and we say that all lost sheep are welcome. We may reach a few, but usually ninety-five percent of the crowd are "found" sheep.

"Why? Because lost sheep are lost and we have to go out and find them.

"Lost sheep often visit places like bars, clubs and discos, and some of us might not want to be seen in these places. People might get the wrong idea about why we were there.

"If Jesus came to Amsterdam," I said to my colleagues, "he would go to the discos. He would know the names of all the bartenders and he would be friends with all the prostitutes. The Bible tells us that Jesus was a friend of sinners; but we may say, 'What about my reputation, my witness?'"

I told the story of how my wife had struck up a friendship with a particular girl with whom she talked about Jesus. "The only way she could see her was to go behind the window and talk with her, while I waited on the street. Men would walk by and think that Jodi was also a prostitute. This made me very angry. But if my wife was going to show God's love to that girl, she had to be willing to be mistaken for a prostitute.

"If you are going to reach lost sheep, you are going to have to be willing to be mistaken for one yourself. Just like Jesus was. He was called a glutton, a drunkard and a sinner. Why? Because he loved them so much he was willing to be mistaken for one himself.

"Jesus was a friend of sinners and I have come to realize that, unless I am too, I am not like Jesus.

"What does the good shepherd do? He leans down, picks up the lost sheep, puts it on his shoulders and carries it home. This is not a clean white fluffy sheep. This is a dirty, smelly sheep. But the good shepherd loves the lost sheep. As the Bible says, 'There is more joy in heaven over one lost sheep that is found, than ninety-nine found sheep.'

"If I am going to communicate God's love effectively, I have first to understand how these lost sheep feel and what is important to them. What are their fears, hopes, cries and dreams?"

I told the group that I believed that Jesus was the supreme communicator. "One day he was walking by the sea and saw a group of fishermen, and he said to them, 'I want to make you fishers of men.' He talked to shepherds and he would say, 'I am the good shepherd who lays down his life for the sheep.' He talked to farmers about seeds and vineyards.

"Jesus communicated in the symbols of the people he was trying to reach. If I said to someone in Amsterdam, 'Did you know that Jesus was the good shepherd?' that person would not have the slightest idea what I was talking about because, as you know, there are not a lot of sheep running around Amsterdam."

After I had delivered this "sermonette," Jodi and I made a conscious decision that we would stop all that we had been doing and would start really trying to get acquainted with the lost sheep of Amsterdam.

This meant giving up an exciting public ministry for something obscure. And it meant that we would do nothing else for a year than go to "lost sheep" places. One particular thing about these lost sheep is they often keep late hours. I knew initially that if I was going to have contact with them, I was going to have to keep lost sheep hours.

Jodi was pregnant with our second son Benjamin, and so I would spend time with my family in the afternoons, but I would be out most of the night.

Our night club team consisted of Barry Johnson and myself. Barry was married to Kay and they had two young children. They came from Florida and were involved in a short-term YWAM summer program; later they felt they should work full-time with Jodi and me.

Barry and I began by spending many hours in prayer. We had all-night prayer meetings twice a month. We would drive out into the countryside and walk and pray in the solitude of the woods, often all through the night.

Usually I had a hard time praying, but when I thought about going to some of those clubs, fear drove me to prayer.

Eventually came the time when God said, "Enough praying! Go!"

So Barry and I found a club where we knew many of the lost sheep hung out—on the weekends, up to 600 of them. We had some red stickers which said, "Smile, God loves you." We thought we would use them to strike up conversations with people in the club.

So, armed with our stickers, we went to The Fizz, an alternative techno-pop discothèque near my home. I had been involved in street evangelism for five years and some Christians considered me to be a radical. But I was in for major culture shock. I couldn't believe how out of touch I was. As we entered the club, I began to feel like Mary Poppins.

We walked towards the dance floor and I looked for some one to give a sticker to. The first thing I began to realize was that it was not cool to have a little red sticker in this place. Multi-colored lights flashed in time with the pounding music.

I saw one young man wearing dark sunglasses freaking out by himself, just jumping up and down in a frenzy in time with the beat.

I thought to myself, *he looks ready.* As he impersonated a pogo stick, I handed him a sticker. Without looking, he took it from me but, as he glanced down at it, he stopped doing his antics and began to scream loudly. I thought to myself, *he must not be ready.*

In the meantime, Barry was sandwiched between two guys who were playfully pushing him back and forth. As I watched I began to wonder if maybe we hadn't prayed enough.

Still, undeterred, I approached someone else and gave him a sticker.

"What is this? Some kind of joke?" he asked as the flashing lights cast eerie shadows across his face.

"No, this isn't a joke. God loves you," I replied.

"Well, I'm not into religion and my family isn't, either."

We talked for the next two hours. Actually what really occurred is that I screamed into his ear and he screamed back into mine.

This was what we did for the next year-and-a-half, and often others would join Barry and me.

It was like going out to war every night.

Later a new member was added to our team. He was Brian Hayes from California. Brian was just eighteen years of age, sported a Mohawk hair style, and wore a long black coat and big leather boots. His hair would often change color during the week, from orange to blond to black. He looked like your archetypal punk, right out of the Sex Pistols era in London.

One day Brian was walking down a street in Amsterdam when he got into a conversation with a couple of kids. "What are you doing here?" they asked.

"Well," he paused. "I'm a missionary."

"You're what?"

"A missionary!"

"Did you change your mind?"

"No, I didn't change my mind," he insisted. "Jesus gave me a new heart."

For the first time these kids realized that having a relationship with Jesus had no connection with which direction your hair pointed. But Jesus had something to do with what's inside a person. They realized Christianity actually is a relationship and, as a result, they got into a deep conversation about knowing Jesus Christ.

Not long after, an additional member joined us, named Roger Bonsack from Norway. We called Roger the "Frankenstein" because he was so large and also because of his black Mohawk and the side of his hair which was dyed blond.

One day we thought we would do something clever to reach those in The Fizz, so we made Roger the sticker man. We put stickers all over the side of his head and plastered them on his clothes.

This huge man, dressed all in black, walked around the bar with the roll of stickers, handing them out to people as we followed behind him, trying to strike up conversations. We had a good time, but it wasn't a very effective way of making contact.

Our strange little team would gather in my apartment for prayer before leaving, and then return, after our nocturnal escapades. Just as dawn was coming up and most of the city was rising from sleep we would pray for those we had contacted.

In The Fizz we talked one-on-one to some 400 people over a period of eight months. We established many relationships with the bartenders, owners and club regulars. Some even came to our home for meals and others asked us to pray for them. I thought I was supposed to go to their clubs to tell them about God, but I learned that the main reason that God wanted us to go was so that they could tell us how they felt, what made them happy, how they saw the future, what their impressions of God were.

I discovered that they were not necessarily closed to the gospel. If they rejected anything, it was my poor communication of it. If I was going to communicate God's love, I had to first of all understand how they felt and what was important to them, what were their fears, cries, hopes and dreams. It occurred to me that this was only being like Jesus.

We would write down the names of everyone we talked to, and then pray for the entire list once or twice a month. We soon began a little Bible study in our apartment for our contacts. This eventually grew to approximately 200 and we developed quite a reputation in Holland.

Among the Dutch Christians we caused great controversy. Some thought we were on the cutting edge of what God was doing, while others thought we were compromising with the world.

It seemed hardly a day went by without a story appearing in one of Holland's newspapers about our night club team.

But it was one of the most respected newspapers in Amsterdam, *Het Parool,* that first called us The Chrunks, meaning the Christian punks.

The YWAM leadership in Amsterdam, however, wanted to close down our ministry because of all the controversy. But Floyd stuck by me and intervened on our behalf.

So we were able to continue. And a slogan on one of our shirts said it all: PUNK'S NOT DEAD. NEITHER IS JESUS.

9
SOUNDS LIKE A FACTORY

I KNEW BY THE DISTRAUGHT EXPRESSION on Barry's face that something was wrong. "We've got to talk. It's very important," he said nervously.

I thought, *Oh no, Brian's in trouble again.* I recalled the time that our most unusual Chrunk had been picked up by the police because of the way he was dressed, and I was afraid it had happened again.

"Is it Brian?" I asked.

"No, it's not Brian," Barry replied.

"It's the mission, isn't it? Who do I need to talk to now?"

"No, it's not the mission," Barry said. "Everything's great with the mission."

"What is it, then?" I was puzzled and I could see that he was having a hard time relaying his news.

Eventually Barry took a deep breath and said, "Kay and I really feel that we're supposed to go back home."

I was stunned. Barry was my right-hand man; I relied heavily on him. He was also one of my closest friends. I knew it had been a difficult year for him and his family, especially for Kay. I was aware that she was often afraid to be alone at home at night with her two little boys. So, even though it was a set-back for me, I understood why they had made this decision to return to the States. Still, I would have to go on without him and sadly, I said goodbye.

Brian and I would train together in the afternoons at a body building gym near our apartment. It was run by a drug dealer and sometimes the guys who worked out there had guns in their gym bags. The owner of the club called us the Missionaries. One time when I was bench-pressing and the weight was too heavy and I needed someone to help get the bar off me, he smiled and said, "Why don't you ask Jesus to help you?"

Because he liked us so much, we normally didn't pay to exercise there. I was getting into the best shape of my life.

After one particularly strenuous session, I was sitting in an outdoor cafe preparing for a Bible study I was to give that night when I felt a sharp pain cut into my side like a surgeon's knife. I'd been having these pains on and off for the past year; my doctor had told me that it was just tension.

I thought that maybe I should go back to the gym and work out, but then came another slicing pain in my side. I got up and somehow staggered home. I stood inside the toilet door, breathing rapidly. Then in excruciating pain, I curled to the floor and rolled myself into a tight fetus-like ball. By now my entire body was shaking and I was drenched in a feverish sweat. I thought I was in the midst of a nightmare.

When Jodi found me, she immediately called a doctor. When he arrived and saw my condition, he cleared his throat and told Jodi solemnly. "Your husband needs to be in a hospital." With that he picked up the phone and called an ambulance.

The next thing I remember was lying in a hospital bed at the AMC Hospital with a profusion of tubes passing through my nose down to my stomach. I felt like I was going to choke. For the next month I was not allowed to eat or drink anything; I was kept alive through intravenous feeding.

It turned out that I had had a bad appendix for about a year. Because it had not been diagnosed correctly, my intestines had become knotted and I had a huge abscess in the lining of my stomach. I discovered later that with this kind of condition I could have died at any moment.

My mother flew in from the States to help Jodi with our two young children, and they would take turns being with me in the hospital. They would try to comfort me in my weakness, as I drifted in and out of consciousness. On one occasion, I awoke briefly to find Jodi gently holding my hand. She forced a smile but her lips trembled. Her face was drawn and tense; her eyes red and swollen.

Brian, whom I had asked to keep the Bible study going, thought it would be a good idea to begin by watching the A-Team on television. Mr. T was Brian's hero and only when the program was over, would Brian begin the study. As a result, fewer and fewer people came, until it had shrunk down to just Brian and Roger, The Frankenstein.

So here I was. I had lost my right-hand man. The Bible study that had been so difficult to start was gone. After nearly a year-and-a-half of going into the bars and clubs, we had hardly anything to show for it.

As I lay in my bed, I felt like I was melting into my pillow. I was so weak I could hardly talk. My eyes had sunk into their sockets and were surrounded by circles so dark it looked like I had black eyes. I got the feeling that Satan was trying to kill me. In an almost delirious state, I thought about my experience with my crippled leg in Yugoslavia. Now, in this present hopeless situation, would I still have faith in God?

With all the strength I could muster, and with tears in my eyes, I prayed out loud: "God, I will *not* give up. I don't care if everybody leaves me. I don't care if I never get out of this hospital, but I will *not* give up. And if I get well again, even if I'm all alone, I'm still going to do what you've asked me to do."

A few days later John Goodfellow came to see me. He had heard that I was sick, but he hadn't realized how serious my condition was. When he saw me, he just broke down and began sobbing. I became aware, in my weakened state, that he was pleading with God to heal me.

As he prayed, I again began to cry, but the miracle he had asked for began to happen. It was extremely slow to start with. I had been in an extremely good condition before I entered the hospital, but now I was so weak, I could hardly take a few steps without fainting. I felt like one awakened from a deep sleep.

I was eventually discharged from the hospital. One day I tried to open our door with my key; I was so weak I couldn't even turn the lock and had to wait for someone to do it for me.

But still, every day, I felt more and more strength gradually returning to my body.

"I think it's now time for you to rebuild your team," John Goodfellow told me one day.

So one by one, new members were added. Briggitte Klumbes from Germany, Michael and Gerry DeJong, Danny Butler and Martijn Krale, all from Holland, as well as many unofficial members.

One day I was with Brian at a rock concert in Amsterdam. He had been telling me for a long time that we needed to start a band and that I should be the singer. I knew this was ridiculous because I had no musical background and I had never sung before. But as we were watching a punk band perform, I was struck by the kind of influence they had on the people attending the concert.

As I watched the band, I had a discussion with God. "You know, God, I'd love to do something like that for you," I said.

And, almost as clearly as I had felt God speak to me when I walked through the university grounds years before this, I felt him saying that I should start a band.

"Brian," I said after the concert, "I think the time has come. We need to start our band."

Danny Butler assured me that he knew how to play the drums. He also had a child's toy drum set. Great! We had our drummer. The only problem was that he had no cymbal stand and he had only one cracked cymbal. So he attached it to a rope nailed to the ceiling. When he hit the cymbal he would have to chase it as it would swing back and forth over his child's drum set.

Frankenstein said he had an old acoustic bass guitar and he found a flat tire inner-tube for the guitar strap. The only problem with his guitar was it wouldn't stay in tune. But it didn't matter. We had a bass player.

Brian, whose hair was white at the time, said he had "found" an electric guitar, and so we were ready for our first rehearsal.

We had a big discussion over what we should call ourselves. Someone who overheard our music said, "That sound is no longer music." I thought, "Great!" So No Longer Music became the name of our band.

The first song that the band wrote was called "The Yeah Song." The lyrics were as follows:

I know what you had to offer us
And it's no good at all;
The same old things throughout the years
Right back to the fall.
No good, no good, no good at all.
At first we had nothing better
Than the things you had to give;
No good, no good, no good at all.
But Jesus came into my life
And showed me how to live.
Yeah! Yeah! Yeah!

During another rehearsal, someone else re-marked that our music sounded "just like a factory." So we named our first demo tape *Sounds Like a Factory*.

John Goodfellow came to one of our practices one day and said, "You guys need to play at the national YWAM staff conference."

We were excited. This was going to be our first big concert. So we put two other songs — "God's not Dead" and "Surprise" — together and we practiced for our big performance.

During the program, Karen Lafferty, a well-known singer songwriter, had just finished singing a beautiful worship song. The audience gave her exuberant applause. Then Karen introduced us and we strutted onto the stage. Frankenstein put the words of our songs on to an overhead screen and drew some strange graphics in with the words. This became standard procedure from then on.

We started into our first song, "The Yeah Song." It was my philosophy back then to have the music as loud as possible so you couldn't hear my vocals very well. To my surprise, some people actually seemed to like our music; others registered great shock on their faces.

We launched into our second song, "God's Not Dead," and it seemed that even more people began to loosen up and get into the music.

We were half-way through our final song, "Surprise" and Brian was doing what he considered to be a stunning guitar solo, when suddenly, a few rows from the front, I saw a man moving from side to side out of rhythm with the band. He then fell forward, taking several chairs with him. He lay on the ground, strangled, glottal sounds coming out of his mouth. Completely shocked, Brian stopped playing his guitar, and I got the attention of Roger and Danny and we stopped in the middle of the song.

As they carried the man out of the hall, we slunk off the stage. You could hear a pin drop. I felt tears of utter frustration sting my eyes.

After the concert, Sally McClung, Floyd's wife, came up to me and said that she felt that our band was of God and that we needed to keep going.

Not everybody felt that way, however, and once again, I found myself at the center of another great controversy. Had the man freaked out because the band had a bad influence on him? Or did he behave in this way because the Holy Spirit was in the band and it was God's influence on him?

Was this new band from God or not? Some people said it wasn't. I wondered who was right.

SINGING
OUT
OF TUNE

IT WAS QUEEN'S DAY, April 30, 1986, the day that Queen Beatrix (with a little help from her loyal subjects) celebrates her birthday in the kingdom of the Netherlands. Amsterdam becomes one huge city party. All the streets are filled with people enjoying this national holiday in a carnival-like atmosphere.

As part of the celebration, live bands play all over the city. Our band was set up to play on one of the main bridges in the city center. We had parked next to us a large van with signs advertising our weekly Bible study which we held on the old houseboats at Steiger (Pier) 14, formerly known as The Ark.

At the bridge, we had a portable electric generator; our band made a thunderous noise throughout the city. Hundreds stopped and listened and were given flyers inviting them to our study.

As we were about to finish our last song, "I Love God," a group of Satan punks, with Mohawk hairstyles, heavy make-up, upside-down crosses painted on their clothes and one with a safety-pin through his cheek, came into view. They stopped beside us and started to scream about how much they hated God and loved Satan. I was shocked to see the real hatred they had for God.

One of them growled and moved menacingly toward me as I was singing and spat in my face. Another took a bottle and broke it over the drum kit and, with his hand bleeding, held it menacingly up to my face.

By this time, a large crowd was gathering and you could feel a violent spirit in the air. I was afraid, but I wasn't going to let this fear control me.

"How many of you believe that Satan is in Amsterdam?" I shouted, my face covered in spit and the angry punk holding the bottle inches from my face.

"We do!" the group of Satan punks shouted back.

"How many of you love Satan," I responded.

"Yes, we love Satan," they said in unison.

You could almost reach out and touch the inflamed tension in the air.

"Well, I have another message," I said. "God is in Amsterdam, too. He loves this city. He didn't just talk about his love, but he proved it by sending his son to die for us. Jesus took our place and died. But he didn't stay dead.

"He rose again from the dead and he's alive tonight in Amsterdam. That's why I'm not ashamed to say I love God in Amsterdam," I continued.

I felt by now that the Holy Spirit was moving.

The guy next to me moved the jagged bottle from my face and smashed it to the ground. A group of them rushed forward and began to slash the tires of our van with knives, while others broke the headlights and windshield. Still others tried to throw us and the equipment into the canal.

Two Dutch policemen arrived on the scene but it was such a flammable situation they had to call for reinforcements before they would even try to intervene. Finally, when more officers arrived, they began to get things a little more under control.

We had thrown as much of our equipment as possible into the back of the van (including Martijn, our sixteen-year-old bass player) and locked the door before they could toss every thing into the canal.

"Drive on!" a police officer told me urgently.

"How can I do that?" I questioned as sweat covered my face. "Three of my tires are slashed!"

"Just drive on," he insisted.

So, with three slashed tires, I drove, or rather limped down the road. The headlights were also smashed and the wind shield wipers bent. We must have looked like quite a sight.

As I drove, people at the side of the road mocked me and shouted, "Jesus!"

I thought to myself, *Are you really stronger, God? Are you really more powerful than the devil?* I didn't feel we were exactly leaving in victory but God was going to teach me something about spiritual warfare that was going to help me in the future.

Two weeks later, we were holding our usual Wednesday night Bible study. At the time, about twenty or thirty people were coming to that meeting. That study grew out of a meeting that Jodi and I had began in our apartment with four kids, and it had become so large it was now held on the house-boats. Our band would always play a few songs and then I would speak.

Suddenly, fifteen Satan punks strode onto the houseboats, led by Raaf. This was his alias, meaning Raven in English. Raaf looked very menacing, his face painted like death with dark, black make-up around his eyes. On his belt was a doll's head with an iron spike through one eye. The others wore chains and some carried big iron hooks that they used to fight with.

They marched in and sat down. Because of our experience on the bridge, we were all terrified, but we were determined not to let that fear stop us.

Our band played a few songs and I began to speak. I told the story of Thomas; how he had doubts about the resurrection; how Jesus appeared to him and said, "Feel my side and my hands."

I said, "Many of you here ask questions about God and have doubts. Jesus wants to prove himself to you tonight just like he did with Thomas!" The power of God was so present that the punks sat quietly for twenty minutes while I spoke. Many of them did not even seem able to look at me.

Afterwards, I tried to talk with some of them and they began to shake physically. I knew it was not because they were afraid, but because of the presence of the Holy Spirit.

I realized that if I wanted to see God's power in my ministry, it was going to cost me something. I thought about the story of Stephen, which I had read in the Book of Acts. He was stoned to death. When Stephen spoke, God's power was so much on his words that the listeners couldn't bear to hear him; they had to cover their ears and scream. I knew that when I spoke on that bridge, God's anointing was upon me, but that the result of walking in God's power could also mean that sometimes I would have to suffer.

The other thing that I learned was what Paul meant in I Corinthians 2:1-5, in which he said:

When I came to you, brothers, I did not come with eloquence or superior wisdom as I proclaimed to you the testimony about God. For I resolved to know nothing while I was with you except Jesus Christ and him crucified. I came to you in weakness and fear, and with much trembling. My message and my preaching were not with wise and persuasive words, but with a demonstration of the Spirit's power so that your faith might not rest on men's wisdom, but on God's power.

I had to understand where my faith was laid—in God's mighty power. My band and I had been so afraid of these Satan punks when they came in that my knees did literally shake and my voice did tremble. I understood that if I was going to be used by God in a great way that I had to be willing to be weak. I knew that God did not want me to live in fear. But he wanted my faith to grow beyond a baby faith that would only do what I felt comfortable or secure in doing.

God wanted me to say to him, "Even when my knees shake and my voice trembles, even when I don't know what to say, help me to obey you."

I also learned never to be ashamed of Jesus. Like Paul, I was starting to understand that there was always power in the message of the cross; I couldn't be ashamed of this message.

The punks finally left and never did cause trouble—which had obviously been their original intention.

People were coming to Jesus almost everywhere we played, and we were soon receiving more invitations than we could handle. Often we would be invited to play with some other band that had albums and years of experience; yet somehow we would end up as the main band.

In a city outside Amsterdam, we were doing a concert for a combination of metalheads and punks. During the concert, one big fat punk was whirling around and knocking people over. Chairs and bottles were breaking all over the hall.

From the beginning, we had made a practice of putting the words of our songs on a big overhead screen so everybody knew what we were singing. When the concert was over I explained why we were there, that Jesus was the answer and that we needed to follow him.

This was not a common message for this crowd, some of whom had written "666" all over our vans in the parking lot.

"Is anybody ready to follow Jesus?" I asked.

"Yo!" a guy yelled from the back and everybody laughed.

I thought, *OK, nobody's interested.*

"If you want to talk, we're available," I said on closing.

The guy from the back of the hall came up to me.

"I wasn't joking," he said. "I want to follow Jesus."

So, with his taunting friends looking on, he gave his heart to God. This sort of thing kept happening all the time.

One time we were doing a concert in a place called The Black Hole. I was told it was a place where Satan lived. After our concert I invited people to follow Jesus. While some of the crowd screamed, "Don't listen, he's a liar," five people came forward and knelt on the stage to receive Christ as their Savior.

I went backstage and was told there was someone who wanted to talk to me. "I heard your message tonight and I wanted to respond," said the man waiting for me. "But I was afraid, because I know what people think about God in this place.

"So I went to a bar and I started drinking this beer," he said, holding up a half-empty bottle. "But the more I drank, the faster my heart started to beat. Tell me what I need to do to become a Christian."

I asked him to pray with me and right there he received Jesus into his heart.

One day I got a phone call. A producer from *Sonja on Monday,* the most popular TV talk show in Holland, told me they wanted the band to appear and Sonja wanted to interview us. Millions of people watch the show and the reason it was so popular was that Sonja would try to make the people she invited look stupid.

She was very anti-Christian, so I knew she would not be a sympathetic interviewer. What terrified me the most was that it was a live program and I would have to do the whole thing in Dutch. My Dutch was only a little better than my singing.

It was very easy for us to have a good prayer time as we prepared for the program. I knew that a lot of people in the Mission were praying, probably more than anything else that No Longer Music would not ruin the Mission's reputation in Holland.

Just as we were about to receive the countdown to start playing, I was so nervous that I thought my heart was going to jump out of my chest. Our bass player, Martijn, wanted to go to the toilet, but there was no time.

Sonja had just introduced us. She began by quoting some lyrics from one of our songs.

Praise God with the compact disc and video, Praise God with guitar and synthesizer, With everything that has breath, praise God.

"These are the words to a song by the Youth With A Mission band, No Longer Music," she said, "and the band sounds like this."

That was our cue to begin. In the studio, the mix of the sound wasn't too bad, but we didn't have a proper PA speaker for the vocals. From what I could tell, I was singing OK.

As I sang the words to our song, the lyrics were projected as sub-titles on to the bottom of the television screen.

The studio audience broke into spontaneous applause. After one song, we came down from the balcony where we had played and I handed Sonja a T-shirt. The name of her program was *Sonja on Monday* and on the T-shirt was printed in Dutch "Sonja on Monday, Jesus Every Day."

She read it out loud and the crowd loved it. After that she asked us different questions and everything seemed to go fine.

Afterwards, we were anxious to talk to people who had viewed the program on TV to find out what they thought. The funny thing was that everybody I would ask would try and change the subject, or say that the interview went well.

Finally, I managed to get hold of a video recording of the program that somebody had made. I discovered that on TV my voice was way out ahead of the music and, to make matters worse, I was singing out of tune.

Shortly after this, I received a postcard. It said, "David, we saw you on *Sonja*. Did you know that you sang out of tune?"

I thought, *God why did you do this? You could have performed a miracle and made my voice good. Maybe sent an angel and made me sing like Amy Grant. At least in tune. God this was your big chance to make the band big. Think of all of the opportunities we would have to preach the Gospel.* I was so humiliated.

I went into a shop and somebody waiting in line stared at me. "Didn't I see you on *Sonja?*" she asked. I thought to myself, *Oh, no, the whole world saw it.*

I went somewhere else in the city, and the person in front of me said to someone next to him, "Hey, look at that guy. He was on *Sonja.*"

I wondered where I could escape. So I went to Amsterdam Zoo. It was Wednesday and I had to prepare for the Bible study. Sitting at the Zoo coffee table, I noticed some people across the room pointing and laughing at me.

God, I said frantically. *I know I can be a proud person and, at times, you need to humble me. But why not in front of a few hundred people or even a thousand? Did you have to do it in front of all of Holland?*

You asked me to sing, so why didn't you help me to sing well?

As I was talking to God and feeling sorry for myself, I felt him speak to me. "I wanted you to sing out of tune, David. You did great; just like I wanted."

But why, Lord? I asked. *Why would you want me to sing out of tune?*

And I felt the Lord say, "Because now when you see what I do, you'll give me the glory, and everyone will know it's me and not your singing."

11
THE FORBIDDEN BAND

It was early Saturday morning, August 8th 1987, when our international team of twenty headed out from Amsterdam to Poland in three rented vans. We had an official invitation from the Polish government and the Baptist church in Wroclaw. Both these invitations were necessary, because Poland was still very much a hard-line Communist country. As Moscow looked nervously on, the leader of Solidarity, Lech Walesa, was locked in a deadly battle with General Wojciech Jaruzelski, the hard-line Polish Communist leader.

It was a four-hour wait at the Polish-East German border. It was obvious that the crossing was designed to intimidate all who passed through. The Polish guards carried automatic weapons and held German shepherd dogs on leashes.

After getting into the country, it took us another six hours to reach our destination, Jarocin, making a total of nearly twenty-four hours' driving. That was quite exhausting for us, especially with our two boys, Aaron and Benjamin along.

Magda, our Polish contact whom we found through someone in Sweden, had arranged for us to travel to Jarocin. It was in this village that the biggest rock festival in Eastern Europe was being held.

I had watched a BBC TV documentary aired in Holland about Polish young people. The program showed the cry that was in their hearts and the hopelessness that was being expressed through their music. During the show they interviewed the lead guitarist and singer from a band called Moscow. (The name was not an indication of pro-Soviet attitudes, but rather a cynical gesture.)

Powel, this guitarist, spoke movingly of his desire for justice and freedom and how their music reflected this desire. When I saw this program, I felt God speak to my heart that we must go to Poland, and that God would get us into that festival.

When we arrived we were full of anticipation. This little Polish village had been invaded by thousands of young people from all over the Eastern Bloc and even the Soviet Union.

What was striking to me was to see Polish priests walking hand-in-hand with the young people, many of whom were hard rockers, heavy metallers and punks. At this time, the Roman Catholic church in Poland, to which 97% of Poland's 38 million people belong, was a bulwark against despair, a sanctuary of freedom, a subversive counterface during a decade of struggle against communist control.

Upon our arrival, we were invited to join a mass for dead rock stars. The priest apparently did this each year; the mass was held in memory of John Lennon, Elvis and others.

There was a procession with people carrying signs with the names of the dead rock stars written on them.

The large Gothic church where the mass was held, was packed solid with young people. That evening we were invited to give a concert and perform our drama on the steps in front of the church.

So with our portable generators set up, we played to about 500 people. We had our songs translated into Polish and projected them onto a screen from an overhead projector.

After we had played, we asked everyone if they would sit down so we could do our drama. The play lasted seventeen minutes and was a reenactment of the fall of man, how Jesus came into the world, how he was crucified and how he rose again from the dead. This was a clear depiction of the gospel with a Polish narration. After it was finished, I stepped out and, with Magda translating, preached about what Jesus did and how he wanted to know us in a personal way.

I invited those who were ready to make this decision to come forward publicly and kneel with me. Hundreds of Polish young people came, many with tears in their eyes, and gave their lives to Jesus. While I was praying with these young people, I looked up and saw hundreds of people linking arms and singing praises to God. It was totally spontaneous — an incredible experience.

The next day we received an invitation to play in the festival itself. There were two stages, the main one that held about 15,000 people and a second one, that held 2,000. We were told that we would be allowed to play on the second stage.

So, rejoicing, we arrived with all our equipment and began setting up. Just before we were about to play, someone in the stage area received a phone call. "No Longer Music (NLM, as some people called us) is forbidden to play," was the terse message.

When I heard this, I protested.

"But we are all set up and the people are waiting for us to play," I said.

"No, you are not allowed to play," we were told. "No foreign bands are allowed in the festival — by order of the government."

Someone overhearing this conversation said to me, "You've got to say something to the crowd," so I went on to the stage.

"We have just been told that it is forbidden for us to play," I said, into the microphone. "But if you want to hear us, we will be playing again tonight in front of the Catholic church."

The fact that we were now the forbidden band suddenly made us the group everyone wanted to see and hear, and hundreds of people left the festival in order to see our concert.

While we played that evening, I recognized in the crowd the guitarist from the band Moscow; the very guy they interviewed on the BBC documentary that I had seen in Amsterdam. He was really into our music and I prayed that he would stay and watch the drama as well. He did and I was glad to see that he was positioned in the middle of the crowd where he could see everything.

After the drama, I again asked those who were ready to make Jesus their Lord to come forward and kneel at the front. Hundreds surged forward. I looked up and caught my breath. There was Powel, and the bass guitarist in the band, Darek Malejonek, kneeling in the crowd. I went up to them and said, "I saw you on the BBC documentary in Holland. I respect your desire to see justice and freedom — how you wish to change Poland."

I paused for a moment, then pressed on. "Music will never change the world. Only God can do that. You need to give your heart to Jesus. With God, you can help change Poland!"

With that, this famous guitarist from one of the biggest rock bands in Poland knelt with me, his guitar hanging on his back, and gave his life to Jesus Christ. The young man I had seen on television, who had so touched me with his heart's cry, was now receiving God's love.

The next day Powel and I met in the main festival and we discussed what his decision meant, what it would cost him. He took me to meet other members of the band. Everywhere we went, young people called out his name and wanted to talk with him. I was amazed to see the influence he had in the country. I linked him with Polish Christians who would disciple him, and he invited us to come back and play in Warsaw sometime.

After the festival, we traveled to Wroclaw to work with a little Baptist church there in an inner city slum. It was one of the worst ghettos I have ever seen outside of Asia. It broke my heart to see children living in such a totally oppressive, ugly and hopeless environment.

We were told that all the alcoholics and criminals lived in this part of the city. The people were extremely poor. We had to drive our vans outside the area to a guarded parking lot. "Otherwise, nothing is safe," one Pole told us.

It is during times like this that I am amazed at the kind of wife God has given me. Jodi never complains or is fearful. We stayed in an apartment right in the ghetto. There were six bolts on our door. I lay in bed and prayed for protection for Jodi, Aaron and Benjamin.

I was invited to preach on Sunday in a little church. I decided to go for a walk and pray about what I should say, while Jodi, the kids and the rest of the team, went sightseeing.

As I was walking and praying, I thought I'd stop in a cafe and have a cup of coffee and read my Bible. It was difficult to find a place to do this in Poland but, from the sign outside a particular establishment, I got the impression that they served coffee. It was about eleven o'clock in the morning and smoke already hung over the table in a blue haze. I noticed some men slumped unconscious, face down on the tables, while others sat there glassily eyeing their drinks. Those still conscious would throw their heads back nervously as they greedily gulped down a clear, hard, fiery liquor which I guessed was vodka.

I could see that this wasn't a coffee-shop so I started for the door. Suddenly, I was grabbed by a half-crazed drunken man, who stared at me in an almost hypnotic state. His face was red, his head newly shaven, and he was built like a fire truck.

"Please let me through," I said, in a firm voice, vainly trying to escape to the exit. Every way I would step, he would get in front of me and block my escape. He then grabbed my arms with two huge swollen hands and started to squeeze them. The pain was intense.

"Jesus," I prayed, "You've got to get me out of here."

Trying not to seem aggressive, I pulled myself free and made a dash for the door, with him in hot pursuit. Just like in the western movies, I was thrown into the street, the door kicked violently shut behind me.

As I picked myself up and dusted myself off, I thought to myself, *Maybe I should give up on coffee!*

Meanwhile, the rest of the team had gone out of the ghetto into another area of Wroclaw. Just as they stepped out of the van, a huge skinhead with a scar on his cheek came up to Brian and tried to rip the earring out of his ear.

Edwin, a guy on our team, intervened and the skin-head gave him a head butt. This all occurred while Jodi and the kids stood there watching.

That evening, in the little Baptist church, I spoke about how God wanted to encourage us to look at his greatness and not our limitations. This was an easy subject for me to speak on because I have clearly seen God use me in spite of my limitations.

Afterwards, I was talking with different people in the church. I spotted an unshaven man in his forties, dressed in tattered clothing, standing in the back of the church. I went up to him and extended a hand of greeting. He seemed moved by my action.

"I want to thank you for being here tonight," he explained through my translator.

"Well, tell me about yourself," I asked.

"You don't want to know about me," he said. "I'm just a simple, ordinary man."

When I heard him say that, I felt a fire rise up inside me and a feeling of God's heart for this man.

"Don't you know," I said, "that God wants to use simple men to change the world?"

If anyone was aware of that, I was. Meeting this man helped me pull together what I believe is God's attitude on our gifts. In 1 Corinthians 1:26-31, I read the following:

Brothers, think of what you were when you were called. Not many of you were wise by human standards; not many were influential; not many were of noble birth. But God chose the foolish

things of the world to shame the wise; God chose
the weak things of the world to shame the strong.
He chose the lowly things of this world and the
despised things — and the things that are not
— to nullify the things that are, so that no one
may boast before him. It is because of him that
you are in Christ Jesus, who has become for us
wisdom from God — that is, our redemption.
Therefore, as it is written: "Let him who boasts
boast in the Lord."

I read that God wants to use the "foolish things of the world to shame the wise."

In Acts 4:13, it says: "When they saw the courage of Peter and John and realized that they were unschooled, ordinary men, they were astonished and they took note that these men had been with Jesus."

What gives God the glory is when we are used in ways we shouldn't be. I found from reading the Bible that God used shepherds to be kings, fishermen to change the world. Too often, I have discovered, I look at my circumstances or gifts and abilities and say to myself, "OK, God can use me within these boundaries." But what gives God the glory is when people say, "I know David Pierce. He could never do that. It must be God working through him."

I believe God is saying today: "Give me an ungifted heart that seeks after me. That's all I need." Often our gifts present a barrier to God because we rely on them rather than God.

After spending a couple of days in Wroclaw, our team traveled on to a drug rehabilitation center in the Polish countryside. Seeing the green grass was a welcome relief after the depressing gray environment of Wroclaw.

Our Polish translator had arranged for us to visit a secular, drug rehabilitation center run by ex-addicts. Those in charge used strict discipline and peer-pressure to help those that came there to kick the habit. Our team of twenty arrived and were met with a skeptical eye and felt a real resistance from the staff to our being there.

On seeing the unfriendly reception, I called the team together. "We need to pray hard that God will soften these people towards us," I said.

We set up our PA system and lights in a meeting room at the center and got ready to do a full concert and drama.

To show their appreciation for the performance, they butchered a lamb and cooked it on an open fire. Under the stars, I talked with one of the leaders of the center. He was a former addict and was built like an ox. He told me that he couldn't believe in God. He said he used to be very violent and he somehow couldn't feel love.

I tried to explain to him the love Jesus had for him; that God wanted to take away his emptiness. While we were talking, I felt an overpowering sense of the Holy Spirit. It was like we were being bathed in a powerful energy of love. It wasn't because of anything we did; it just happened and we both could feel it at the same time. This big, tough man began to cry. Tears rolled uncontrollably down his cheeks. He could not deny God's presence any longer and we prayed together.

Life, he knew, would never again be the same. When we left the center, many conversions like this had taken place. It was an incredible time; a special bond had developed between us and many tears were shed on both sides. We had been raised under different ideologies, but our needs were exactly the same. We all needed love — God's love in our lives.

We would now travel to Jarocin, Poland. The government allowed this festival to take place because it also celebrated the pilgrimage to the Black Madonna in Jasna Gora. Millions of Poles went there on this religious excursion every year. It was said that the painting of the Black Madonna had saved Poland in a battle and it possessed certain healing powers. By being there the people were registering a form of political protest and solidarity against the communist government.

Jarocin was full of campers and one particular camp site housed a famous hippie group. It was a large area where thousands of young people camped out, listened to music, smoked hashish and visited the Black Madonna. It was a strange sight.

The priest in charge of the area was known as the Hippie Priest. He held giant masses on the field, mixing Catholicism, New Age and the occult. When we arrived, I felt I should request to be under his authority, and then I asked if we could perform a concert on the open field.

My request to be under the priest's authority stemmed from something we had learned working a few years earlier in the red light district of Amsterdam. Our team would go at night to one of the most dangerous streets, preach and then invite people to our coffee house. One night, while we were doing our coffin sketch, a riot nearly broke out as the prostitutes began screaming at us from across the canal. Before I knew it, I was surrounded by bouncers hired to control things in the neighborhood. They were all trained kick-boxers and were extremely violent.

Alex, one of the Dutch bosses of that street, was pushing me while I was surrounded by his boys. The rest of our team was nowhere to be seen, except for Jodi, who vainly tried to reason with Alex.

"Shut up! I'm the boss here!" he told Jodi.

"Let me explain," I said.

"Shut up! I'm the boss here," he repeated.

Jodi and I got the message, so we picked up the coffin and left for our coffee house. I was shaking from the experience, but I knew God wanted us to go back there. Jodi felt the same prompting, too, but she also didn't want me to go back there because she thought something terrible would happen to me — I might even get killed. So our little team prayed and cried out to God for his solution to our dilemma.

While we prayed, I felt a strong impression that God was saying to me, "Go back and ask Alex's permission." I told the team to wait and I walked back alone to the same street where I thought Alex might be. There he was, in front of one of the brothels, talking to one of the girls.

"Hello, Alex," I said in as calm a voice as I could muster. He was startled to see me, especially as I was alone. "I would like to ask you something."

The vice boss glared at me. "OK, what is it?," he said impatiently.

"Could I have your permission to come back here tomorrow night and have a street meeting on the bridge?" I said.

After a few moments of eye-to-eye dueling, he replied brusquely, "Sure, go ahead. After all, I'm the boss here." He then turned his face up to the sky, appearing to consider it for rain.

The next evening, we returned and sang and preached on the bridge and nobody bothered us this time, not even the police. (The police are often paid off by guys like Alex.)

So, I thought, if I put myself under the authority of the priest, like I did with Alex, we could get a positive response. The Hippie Priest, like Alex, said, "Sure you can have a concert," and allowed us to set up in the best position on the field, where there was a natural incline.

It was the perfect place for a concert — until it started to rain. We parked our two vans alongside each other and put a tarpaulin up between them. About a thousand young people gathered in the pouring rain.

After the concert and drama, I preached. I told about how we needed to be born again, how Jesus died on the cross but now was risen from the dead. How he took our place and how we needed to repent of our sins. I tried to make it as difficult as possible for people to respond. I said, "If you're ready to give your hearts to Jesus and make him the King of your life, come forward right now!"

A sea of young people immediately surged forward. During the next four hours, our team and a Polish Baptist youth group who had come from Wroclaw to be with us, prayed with many young people to receive Christ into their lives.

The Hippie Priest was deeply moved with what had occurred on his patch. "Please come back again," he said. "Because you are here, we have really felt God's presence and his love!"

We embraced and I said that we would love to come back. Exhilarated, but totally exhausted, we started our thirty-six hour trek back to Amsterdam.

The forbidden band was forbidden no more!

NO LONGER MUSIC & TEQUILA PARTY

Entering Christiania was like walking into a bizarre underworld. Leaving the relative affluence and orderliness of Copenhagen, we were transported back into an alternative city-state of people who had opted out of the system.

As I walked through the front gates of Christiania, I was confronted by open-air tables set up everywhere with drug dealers selling huge blocks of hash. People staggered from the effects of alcohol and other drugs. Parents walked together with their children as they smoked from a hash pipe.

Taking pictures there was prohibited, but the most powerful feeling I got was that of a highly-charged, spiritual atmosphere of darkness.

It's hard to believe that this hold-over from the hippie age still exists. Christiania was established in the sixties as a free sector of the inner city of Copenhagen where drugs would be freely available and an alternative society was to be formed, with its own laws and police. It also has its own factories and business operations, including the largest drug-dealing network in Scandinavia, and its own beauty shops. If you got your hair cut in one of these establishments, they will also straighten out your energy aura at the same time.

Christiania is run by organized crime, biker gangs, leftist squatters and the remnants of the Sixties hippie culture.

Thousands of young people go there to buy drugs. Many of the children of the original inhabitants have grown up in the scene and have created a second generation who only know this counter-culture. Whenever the Danish government has tried to close down Christiania, there have been huge protests from many of the "normal" people in the city who appear to admire those living there.

In a battle of policy, the Danish government has been upset with Sweden over a nuclear power plant near their border. I was told that Sweden would consider closing down the plant only if the Danes would also close down Christiania. But the Danes were afraid to do this because they know that it would mean warfare, and the police are afraid to even enter Christiania unless they are in riot gear, and even then only in large numbers.

Christiania was to be one of the two places we had been asked to perform in during July of 1988. (The other was the Black Horse, a squatter fortress in Copenhagen, where terrorist groups like the Palestine Liberation Organization and the Provisional Wing of the Irish Republican Army were being trained.)

What the organizers of our visit had failed to mention to the people who now ran these places was that we were Christians. When I heard of this oversight, I was alarmed. After praying, I prepared to meet with the leaders of both groups to tell them that a Christian band was scheduled to play in their clubs. I knew this would be dangerous, but I also was aware that it had to be done. It would be even more hazardous to say nothing and let them discover we were Christians the moment we played. That could provoke a riot—or worse!

So Brian, Rene (the organizer) and I went to Christiania to meet with Fleming, a bar owner, who had set up our concert there. It was scheduled for the roof of one of the main bars there called Nemo Land. This place was established by a biker gang that had fought against the local Hell's Angels. Fleming was part of this gang and had attended twelve funerals of friends of his gang. He himself was nearly killed in five fights.

Fleming was a well-built blond man with a rock-solid body which I guessed had come from disciplined weight training. He also wore a long pony tail. After shaking hands with him, Brian, Rene and I sat down at a table.

"Hey, you guys, do you want a beer?" he asked in a friendly fashion.

"No thanks, Fleming," I said nervously.

He eyed me suspiciously.

"Fleming, I owe you an apology," I told him, deciding to plunge straight into the business at hand.

He gave me a quizzical look.

"When this concert was organized, Rene wasn't completely honest with you and I believe that was not right," I continued. "We are Christians. We sing about God, Jesus, and say that there is hope. I think you should know that."

The burly man nearly fell off his chair. He then looked at Rene whose face had by now turned a whiter shade of pale.

"Are you a Christian, too?" he asked pointedly.

Rene nodded.

"How old are you?" Fleming asked and, before Rene could reply, he jabbed in with another question, "Does your mother know you're here?" With that he let out a huge bellow of laughter and ordered up some fruit juices for us.

"Do you only sing about God?" he asked, leaning back in his easy chair.

"Yes," I said. "We sing about God, about how there is a future. Do you think they would like that here?"

Fleming paused for a moment and then allowed a slight smile to cross his face. "Well, as long as you don't sing 'Hallelujah' all the time," he chuckled, "that will be all right."

"We won't do that," I promised.

I then inquired if a Christian band had ever played before in Christiania.

"Are you kidding?" he said, standing up. Finally, he extended his hand to me and said, "OK,

David we'll do it."

From there, we went to the Black Horse. This was a completely different type of community, one that specialized in violence, especially with the local police. When we arrived at this large, red-brick building, surrounded by a ten-foot high brick wall, we discovered the only way you could get in was through an ominous iron gate.

The place was under twenty-four-hour surveillance by the Copenhagen police and anyone who went in had their picture taken by a police officer equipped with a telephoto lens.

When we arrived I noticed that by the iron door was a shopping cart full of bricks, presumably to throw at the police if the need arose.

To enter the main squatter building, you had to dial a computer code. As I went through the door, I realized that these guys were real terrorists, not just rebellious young people. A police shield that they had won in a street battle leaned against a wall of the room I was ushered into.

Posters hung on the walls depicting violent confrontation and revolution. One said, "PLO and IRA: fighting for the same cause."

We sat down with Rasmus, one of the leaders there. He got straight to the point.

"Is it true that you are Christians?" he asked. The word had gone out and they had heard only a few hours after we had talked with Fleming in Christiania.

"Yes," I said. "You should have been told that right away. I'm sorry that this has happened."

"No problem," said Rasmus, "but you might have some trouble when you play. Some of the people here are anti everything."

I handed him a cassette of our music and he read the lyrics to some of our songs. "These are cool," he said as he checked them out.

He led Brian and myself to the bar where we would be playing. It was like a lot of bars we had been in before, except for one major difference. The door had half a dozen iron bars across it so that it would be impossible to get through once it was closed.

We were scheduled to play in this bar on Thursday night, and Christiania on the following evening.

Rasmus revealed that there would "likely be trouble" on Thursday night at the Black Horse, so our team gathered and prayed together that if God wanted us there, he would keep that door open. If not, he would firmly close it. If God kept the door open, we would go regardless of the consequences.

We agreed that we were going to play there unless we were physically barred from the building.

I thought of the story in Daniel chapter three. King Nebuchadnezzar made an image of gold and said that those who did not fall down and worship this idol would be cast into a fiery furnace.

Three men—Shadrach, Meshach and Abednego—refused, and told Nebuchadnezzar, "O king...we will not serve your gods or worship the image of gold you have set up."

I felt that God was asking us if we were prepared to go into the fiery furnace, even if we weren't to be delivered from it. The question was, were we? I thought we were, but it was a terrifying prospect.

We had a whole day to wait before the concert, and so we gathered again together to pray. To make things worse many in our team were reading scriptures about martyrdom and being willing to die for Jesus.

I called up Jodi on the phone in Amsterdam and told her what the situation was. As I expected, she felt we were doing the right thing. I went for a long walk and tried to imagine what it would be like to die in this club if somebody stabbed me. I felt almost physically sick from the fear that consumed me.

But still I told God that I was not going to back down.

It was now 6:30 p.m. and time to set up the equipment in the Black Horse. As our team arrived to do this, they were confronted by two raging women.

"This is a very angry place," one of them shouted. "Why do you want to play here? Do you want to die?"

Brian was nervous and was shaking so hard he could hardly stand up. He tried to explain that we had permission from Rasmus to play, but that didn't seem to satisfy them.

"We don't care," said the woman. "We hate Christians. We hate you and we will kill you. If you play here tonight it will be suicide for you."

Then our drummer, Peter Zaal, bravely interjected, "Maybe. But we are willing to take the risk."

With a steel-like sense of purpose, the team tried to move the equipment through the door, but before they could get close, a guy slammed the door shut and locked it. So God closed the door literally and protected us from certain violence. A little shaken up, we gathered together and thanked God for his safekeeping and prayed for those lost in the Black Horse.

On the next night, we moved on to Christiania. We arrived at four in the afternoon for our set-up. I talked with Fleming and he told me he had heard what had occurred at the Black Horse and said that we could have played at his place on Thursday night as well.

"Those guys there are crazy; they're real killers," he exclaimed. Coming from this man, I knew this was no exaggeration.

Another band played before us called the Body Bags. They weren't exactly Christian. With much fear and trembling we prepared to play next. What we hadn't realized was that Fleming had advertised all over the city that there was going to be a No Longer Music and Tequila Party. They had built a huge bonfire outside the bar and people were already drinking bucketful's of tequila.

When we finally took the stage, we were greeted by cheers, screams. Many didn't even know we were there because they were so drunk or "zoned out" on hashish.

The crowd for the outdoor concert had grown by now to nearly 400 people. We played for three hours and I made a statement: "I want to say what a privilege we feel it is to play here and I want to give a special thanks to Fleming for his help," I said.

I told them that I had taken a walk that day around their lake and I understood their desire to have more than the world offered them.

"But there is someone here today who loves this place, and that's God," I declared. "God loves Christiania and he wants to be your friend and he wants you to be truly free. That's why he sent Jesus to show us the way."

When he heard the word "Jesus," one guy began screaming at me. Fleming shouted to him in words that I can't repeat, that if he didn't sit down he would be sorry. The man got the message and quieted down.

Different people in the crowd later said they loved the words of the songs that we projected on a screen, but were amazed that a Christian band could play there.

Fleming asked us to come back in October. A member of the Body Bags also asked if we could play with them and some other bands at a later date.

During our time in Copenhagen, we also performed our drama on the streets and preached to the assembled crowds, and I was interviewed on Danish TV. We realized what a miraculous door had opened in Christiania, but I'm continuing to learn that God performs miracles for all those who obey him.

Since then we've been to Christiania on several more occasions and my relationship with Fleming has grown even warmer.

On one visit, Fleming arranged for us to play in another bar in an infamous drug-dealing street in Christiania.

"When it comes to discrimination, we're the same," I shouted between songs. "In Amsterdam, we've been banned from playing in some of the clubs there because of what we stand for. People have been against us because we don't go along with the system they want us to follow," I continued.

"We follow Jesus and, like you, people discriminate against us because we are saying something different."

The crowd at that point wasn't sure how to react. They liked to talk about how they were being persecuted by the system because they were alternative or different. Yet they didn't want to recognize our right to also be alternative.

"The good news for Christiania is that God is not just an energy or a force," I continued, "but a

Father with a broken heart whose son, Jesus, rose from the dead."

Suddenly screams could be heard from inside the bars as we performed on the street. Although it was a potentially violent situation, I felt God's all-embracing peace as I spoke.

Later, our YWAM worship band, Masterpiece, played and sang different praise songs. Terry, a former brawler and street fighter from England, spoke about how Jesus can forgive us for anything we've done and he himself was living proof of it.

There was reaction from the crowd, both negative and positive, as he spoke, and then suddenly, the electrical power went off.

Someone in their anger had cut the chord to the PA system with a knife so we figured that meant the concert was now over.

Later a girl told me that her heart had ached when we played because of the spirit she felt in our music.

Fleming told me that we were always welcome to play in Christiania.

That same trip, our band played during Carnival. This wild celebration is held in the city-center of Copenhagen and is a time when the inhabitants get insanely drunk and riots often take place between drunken Danes and Swedes. The gutters are literally awash with a mixture of beer and urine.

My eldest son Aaron, who at this time was nine years old, was with me on this trip. It was my practice to bring Aaron and Benjamin with me as often as possible on these tours. As a result, they expected to see God do great things. While the equipment was being set up in a square, I took Aaron to a nearby burger bar to eat.

Several huge bouncers stood at the entrance. The city was full of drunken people, many with their faces painted. Even the burger bar was in need of bouncers during the revelry. In fact, later on that evening, our guitarist and Masterpiece's drummer were returning from a Christian coffee house. While crossing a street, they were attacked by a group of drunken Swedish guys who, for no apparent reason, started to beat them up. Fortunately, they weren't seriously hurt, only shaken.

As we began the outdoor concert, a strange crowd gathered to listen. They were a combination of drunken people and local Christians. Many of those watching screamed obscenities or threatened us with their fists as I spoke of Jesus.

Yet again I felt a complete confidence and authority from God. At first I didn't feel the urge to speak, but I thought I might as well give God a chance to touch the people standing there. I didn't expect much from such a crazy crowd. I would often involve my sons when I spoke and I felt I should do this now with one of them.

"I want you to meet my son, Aaron," I said. My little boy walked through the crowd to me and I put my arm around him. "I care about my son and I think he has value. I love him and will defend him to the end. I want good things for my little boy and nobody better say anything bad about him because I will not stand for it," I shouted.

"God is a good father, too, and he is concerned for us and he wants to know us like I know and love my little boy." I then gave Aaron a hug.

"He wants to pick us up in his arms and comfort us and forgive us for all the bad things we've done. So he sent his son Jesus to show us the way back."

When the crowd heard the name Jesus, some mocked and shouted at me. But I continued to explain how God wanted to save us.

"If you want to know Jesus," I concluded, "I invite you to kneel with me on this street and we will pray together."

I knelt down and immediately, four young men and a young woman, all in their twenties, came forward. Together we huddled on the street, Aaron and I and these five Danes. As we cried out to God drunks stood over us, ridiculing the group. The woman was by now crying and others looked on intently as I led them in prayer.

A group from a Danish church from Copenhagen who were working with us, later said that the hardest people to the gospel they had ever known were Danish youth.

"This is the first time we've ever seen any Danish young person receive Christ publicly on the streets of Copenhagen," I was told.

God had once again moved in a supernatural way as I stood back and watched in awe! He had again used his flawed and fragile servant.

13

LETHAL GOSPEL

As our rented diesel van headed off, I felt my spirits lift. We were leaving the overcast gloom of Amsterdam for the sunshine of Spain.

"It's going to be great," said Brian. "We'll just do concerts and then hang out on the beach."

Olaus, our Norwegian sound man, started to flex his muscles, imagining himself standing on a beach surrounded by adoring admirers.

We were en route to Bilbao, to help with a new work in the city. But what we hadn't realized was that Bilbao, capital of the Basque region of Spain, was also home of the Basque separatist organization known as ETA, which wants no collaboration with the Spanish state, but an independent Basque state.

The armed revolutionaries of ETA are much like the IRA Provisionals in Northern Ireland. They are supported by the communists and trained by well-known international terrorists. There was a long history of oppression and injustice against the Basque people which has given the opening for a terrorist organization like ETA to operate.

In Bilbao, and other parts of the Basque region, there are youth clubs. These clubs are designed to encourage young people to join the ETA group.

As our van swung into this ancient city, Brian shouted, "Hey, isn't this great. We can at last be a real rock band doing concerts when people aren't trying to kill us." I hadn't seen Brian so "up" for quite some time.

The leader of the work in Bilbao sat down with us and enthused, "Man, we've got some great concerts lined up for you."

"Fantastic. Where are they?" I smiled.

He paused for a moment and then replied, "They're in these terrorist clubs!"

Brian and Olaus exchanged shocked glances.

He then drove us to a part of the city where one of the leaders of these clubs was based. The person we were to meet was called Sante.

Brian and I were introduced to him and our host asked Sante if he would like to have a band from Amsterdam play in the biggest youth club in Bilbao. He handed him a cassette of the music and said casually, "By the way, they're Christians."

Sante appeared startled. A Christian band to perform in an ETA youth club. If we were allowed to play, it would be the first time ever. During the long and brutal fascist reign of General Francisco Franco, the Roman Catholic church collaborated with the oppressive government and were party to many of the injustices of the period. So in the minds of ETA, Christians were the same as fascists. They associated us with injustice and bondage. They were encouraged in this belief by their communist brothers. So we know that if we were given permission to play, it would be a great miracle.

We left without Sante making any firm commitment. So we gathered together and prayed fervently. It's amazing how you pray when you know the consequences could be threatening personally, that your very life could be in danger. These situations have a way of stripping away all the polite religious interceding we often do. We had come to understand only too well the significance of playing in these clubs. These guys were killers. Sometimes, we heard, they would assassinate people in the city. One method we were told about was to run up to joggers, pull out a concealed hand-gun and shoot the person in the head at point-blank range.

Our prayer was that God's will would be done regarding this situation. We were prepared to go into the lions' den if God wanted us to do so. But only if he called us. The lions' den without God's angels could be very dangerous.

The pressure-cooker situation caused many problems for us; and Jodi, who was with us on the trip and made it a lot more bearable for me, was fed up with certain band members complaining and sometimes acting like complete jerks. On the trip down, there had been some arguments over who sat where in the van, or a band member would talk rudely to another member of the team.

"David, we have to have a band meeting," she said one day.

I knew by the tone of her voice that we were all in big trouble.

"We need to make things right, or we are going to stop God from being able to use us at all on this trip," she said.

During the gathering, different members of the team felt convicted of bad attitudes they had had towards each other and there was a time of making things right. We realized how important our unity was at a time like this.

Surprisingly, Sante not only agreed to our playing in the club in Bilbao, but he was also going to arrange for us to play in two others as well. We couldn't believe it. And as an added bonus, they were going to pay us!

I savored the thought that a terrorist organization was going to pay us to sing about Jesus in their clubs.

The day came for our first concert. We still hadn't seen the beach but instead had spent most of the time praying that we wouldn't die. When we arrived in the village we found the youth club. I was told that ETA people would normally go to a village, find a building they liked, and forcibly take it over. Because of who they were, people in the village would be intimidated and never objected.

We entered the hall with our equipment and were greeted by the less-than-friendly members of the club. The place had a spirit of violence about it. I found it difficult even to breath inside the place, it was so oppressive.

Murder, rebellion, anarchy and anti-Christ messages were scrawled on the walls around the club.

One picture was of President Reagan with blood pouring from his mouth.

The band that would play before us was called Lethal Gospel. Their message was the complete opposite to ours. At first I thought it would be hard for us to play with bands like this. But I eventually came to see it was the best thing that could happen. It was as if God wanted to show everybody who had the real authority.

People watched them play, mildly interested, standing outside while they performed inside the hall.

Jodi and I sat in a cafe across the street before the concert. I kept wondering what they would do when they discovered that we were singing about Jesus, especially as we knew they were violently anti-God. But I also knew that God had arranged for our being there. We were about to enter the lions' den, but I was confident that Jesus was going to be there with us.

When Lethal Gospel completed the set, we climbed on the stage and started our concert with a worship song, "I love you, Lord, and I lift my voice," which I sang a cappella.

Then we launched into our first band number and the power of God came down. People who were just hanging around outside rushed in to listen. I felt not only God's protection, but also an authority and righteous anger against all the lies that had been proclaimed in that place.

Jodi later said that my message that night was the strongest she had ever heard me preach. God's Spirit had so broken through in the place that the heavy spirit in the hall had disappeared. It now felt like you could have even held a church service in the place.

The second village hall we played in was even heavier than the first. I felt like we were in a snake pit. A picture of a terrorist executing a policeman was the backdrop for the stage. On the walls were slogans like, "You can kill the Revolutionary, but not the Revolution!"

The band that played before us made Lethal Gospel look quite innocent. They were a thrash, hardcore punk band that basically played one note with a lead singer who screamed at the top of his lungs.

Again, after much prayer, we took the stage. We began the concert on our knees this time. The whole band sank to its knees as we played "Humble yourself in the sight of the Lord." Just like in the other club, God gave us a real authority.

People who were drinking outside again came in to listen. A spirit of joy replaced the heavy spirit that was there before we played. The audience even asked us to play several encores. It was a tremendous breakthrough. We felt honored to see God doing such mighty things.

We prepared to play the final time in the main youth club in the Bilbao. Each club seemed heavier than the last. This was certainly the worst. From a pillar hung a statue of the Virgin Mary with a noose around her neck. A sign read, "Every day, when you get out of bed, you must say, 'I defecate on God.'"

Other blasphemous and anarchistic symbols adorned the walls of the club. The place had a horrible smell because it had just been fumigated for fleas. The toilets were overflowing dark holes in the back of the building.

I felt like we were preparing to perform in the devil's living room. The band that played before us was another thrash punk band. The atmosphere was again heavy and down, but because of our experiences in the other two clubs, we were full of faith and expectation.

As in the previous clubs, it was good that another, totally opposite band played before us, because I felt it showed everybody who had the real power. Again, a spirit of joy and peace entered the hall and the organizer of the club was so impressed that he said we were welcome back and he would organize concerts for us in the clubs run by this terrorist organization at any time.

We did finally make it to the beach, but only once!

In February of the next year, we prepared to return. After an eighteen-hour drive from Amsterdam, we again arrived at the terrorist youth club in Bilbao that we had previously performed at. When we got there I noticed a distance in Sante that wasn't there before. He seemed afraid to talk with us. This time their council was there and the people seemed more confrontational.

We took down the statue of Mary with the rope around her neck, so that we could put up a sheet on which to project our words. This made one of the people there especially angry. He demanded we turn off the overhead projector, but we refused.

The hall was soon packed solid. As we played, some people shouted and wrote obscene things on the walls against God. But still He protected our team from violence.

But I felt a little uneasy about something. Then God revealed to the band and to me that a subtle pride had been creeping into our attitudes. Because of our past victories, we weren't seeking God with all our hearts. We had felt a confidence that wasn't in God, but in ourselves.

Our team prayer time beforehand was too relaxed. We became confident in ourselves. We had a band meeting and different ones spoke about these attitudes. After a time of repentance and prayer, God started to move again and we were greatly encouraged. We were invited for a thirty-minute radio interview and I was able to explain how NLM had a different message from most bands and that Jesus offered hope.

The next day we played in what was known as the worst heavy-metal bar in Bilbao. It was a tremendous evening and the bar was packed solid. The owner was touched and he came to a Sunday church service the next day where I spoke. Afterwards he took my hand and asked if we could please come back.

"Anytime you're in this city, you're welcome to play here," he said.

We had played in the devil's living room and God had given us the victory.

14
A CITY WITHOUT HOPE

WAVES OF EXHAUSTION WASHED OVER ME. We had driven non-stop overland from Amsterdam to Moscow and hadn't really slept for three days on that seemingly never-ending journey to the Russian capital.

A domestic Aeroflot jet now carried us from Moscow to Alma-Ata, deep in Soviet Central Asia. The plane was packed and it wasn't easy to sleep, crammed as I was against the window with no place to put my legs and someone's knees jammed into the back of my seat.

I finally gave up on sleep and began to reflect on the events that had led up to this historic moment. While our band had played in front of the church in Poland during our first tour there, Marek, a music promoter, had stood quietly watching us. He had recently been released from prison after apparently being falsely accused of some shady business deals. In the totalitarian rule of Poland at that time, the authorities deemed there was no need for a trial, so he was imprisoned without ever appearing in court.

Magda, our Polish translator, who was a prison visitor at the time, had met him inside and began talking to Marek in his cell. After a while she led him to Christ. After watching our band perform, Marek asked if he could be our manager in that region of the world.

I agreed, and he immediately began organizing this tour for us through Soviet Central Asia and Siberia. This was before the collapse of communism and many of these cities in which we were to perform were previously closed to the gospel. No Christian band had ever played there before.

On that flight in April 1990, I was feeling more insecure than normal. I also had some doubts about the maturity of our new band. This feeling wasn't dispelled when I saw our new drummer bring his favorite blanket and pillow with him on the plane.

The break-up of the old band had saddened me.

Brian had fallen in love with a Norwegian girl who attended our weekly Bible study in Amsterdam on the houseboats. They had decided to get married and had felt they should spend some time together in Norway.

Martijn was also planning to get married and had left the band as a result.

And Peter Zaal, the drummer, moved back to the Dutch countryside with his wife who was pregnant with their first child.

I realized that girls had been a definite threat to our old band, but as I looked around the plane, I took comfort in the fact that, with the group I had now, I wouldn't have to worry about this: no girl would ever want to talk to them.

So with the new band we started our arduous trip to Alma-Ata. We would be performing in two Soviet Islamic republics, Kazakhstan and Kirghizia, and from there we would head for Siberia. The excitement of going to these unreached areas was tempered by the thought of being separated from my family for a month.

Another concern I had was that the translator I was counting on was not able to travel with us, and the other translator we had was not that good. His assistant, a Polish guy, couldn't speak Russian or English. So we were starting the tour with only one translator, and a poor one at that, with his helper only speaking Polish. We ended up calling him The Camel, because all he could do was carry things and no one could communicate with him, the Russians, or us.

Keith, whom I invited to come along to help and be an assistant road manager, was still trying to come to terms with the fact that he had the AIDS virus. Now, a year-and-a-half later, Keith was a transformed, on-fire evangelist, but was also aware of this terrifying time-bomb ticking away inside of him.

God knew that on this trip I could only trust in him; not in myself, the band or the organizers. I was truly operating in complete weakness. But as I prayed on the trip to Moscow, I felt God had me in the perfect place, so that he could show me just how mighty and powerful he really was. A conviction grew in my heart that, despite the difficulties, this trip was going to be truly supernatural.

Our first stop, Alma-Ata, the capital of Kazakhstan, was located 100 miles from the Chinese border. What made the situation even more extraordinary was the fact that our concerts were being arranged by Muslim music promoters. I was pleased that all our literature had safely made it through the borders. Stuffed together with all of our sound equipment were thousands of donated Russian gospel tracts, hundreds of Bibles, study Bibles, hymn books and teaching tapes.

It was the first time that I had worked in an Islamic area, and we had been warned by expert organizations in Holland that, while working in the Muslim world, we should not be too bold. I was warned by them to take it easy, but I still felt we should project the words to our songs on a screen in Russian. This in itself would be confrontational, especially since the lyrics spoke clearly about Jesus Christ, the cross and sin.

We initially planned to just play our music and talk with people after the concert, but while we were preparing I thought, *What would it hurt to throw the Russian tracts into the crowd while we played?* Keith also decided to make some Russian signs to show the audience. So we gradually slipped farther and farther away from taking it easy.

Everything possible went wrong during our first concert in Alma-Ata. Guitar strings broke in the middle of songs; props and electrical equipment broke down; and yet I felt a tremendous sense of God's power as I stood before the large crowd.

During one song, I ran around the audience throwing Russian booklets, and people literally dived for them and began reading them. I stopped in the middle of the concert and said, "God's not dead, is he?" and Keith came on stage carrying a large sign with "Nyet!" written on it. So I'd say again, "God's not dead, is he?" and Keith would hold up the sign and the audience would enthusiastically shout "Nyet!"

Here we were in the Soviet Union in an Asian Republic and a crowd of mainly Muslim young people were shouting in effect, "God's not dead!" I felt tears well up in my eyes at this moving moment.

After the concert, hordes of young people wanted the band members to sign their Russian booklets that explained in detail everything they needed to know about having a relationship with Jesus.

Backstage, Keith talked with one of our Muslim promoters. He pointedly asked this lady, "Do you want to give your life to Jesus?" She indicated that she did and so he prayed with her.

During our second concert, it was difficult for me to sing because I was overwhelmed with a desire to weep for the people. I told them, "God loves Alma-Ata," and "Jesus is the answer to our problems." We gave away hundreds of Bible tracts to people that night, including the military police, who were in high-profile attendance to keep order.

Our third concert in the city took place on Easter Sunday. In the morning, I had visited the pastor of a Baptist church and was able to give him some Bibles and money.

We invited a Russian band to play a song before our concert. During our performance, I felt I should this time clearly explain the gospel and call for a public response. I knew I was going against all the expert advice that I had been given, but I somehow couldn't help myself. I told the people how God loved them and how he cared about hate and injustice.

"God sees all the injustice in our world and wants to bring justice to it," I declared.

I then went on to say that we had turned from God and made man a god. To this Muslim audience, who had probably never heard this message before, I told how Jesus came and died and rose again for us.

"Because of this we can know God personally, like a true friend," I affirmed.

I then invited people to respond publicly if they needed forgiveness and this friendship with God.

"If you would like to know Jesus, please come and kneel with me on the stage," I asked. Ten people came forward, including the entire Russian band. They faced the audience, with the spotlight in their faces, declaring their new-found faith.

We took all those who had responded backstage and gave them Bibles, explaining what it meant to follow Jesus, and then gave them the address of the local Baptist church.

Other members of the band prayed with many people that night. Some of them also went into the audience and talked one-to-one with people, while others met with those backstage who came forward.

The next day Keith told me that we needed to meet. I could tell by his expression that it was something serious. I walked in a room where the rest of the band had gathered.

Russell began first. "I just don't feel right about going on to Frunze," he grumbled. "The organizer told me that they haven't sold any tickets and I just don't feel good about it."

Keith then pitched in. "It just doesn't make any sense," he said. "Instead of going there, we could spend our time here."

I looked at The Captain. "Do you feel the same way, too?" I asked.

He nodded his head.

I suppose I could understand why the band felt this way. We had done concerts before that had been poorly organized and they had turned out to be complete disasters. But still I felt on this occasion that what they were saying wasn't right.

"This is an unreached city," I pointed out. "Of course we're going to have problems if we go there, but I think we will be making a huge mistake if we don't go."

I could feel the tension rise in the room. "We need to pray again about this," I said bluntly.

After a time of prayer, I pulled rank and said, "We're going and I hope you can feel good about it."

I hoped that I was right and felt a sense of disappointment about what had occurred, but we headed off for Frunze, the capital of Kirghizia, which was settled by Chinese Muslim refugees before the Soviets took power there in 1918.

When we arrived, our Muslim guide explained that this was a city without hope. She said that the people there didn't believe in Mikhail Gorbachev's policy of *glasnost* (openness).

"Their hero here is an author who wrote that suicide was the only answer to their despair," she went on, and continued her tale of woe by adding that there was little food or clothing in the shops. "Children here are mistreated and forced to go to nurseries," she said. "Life is rigid and controlled. The people have no space in which to create or to feel fulfilled."

The "high class" hotel for foreigners that we were checked into had no hot water—and the cold water came out a strange, brown color.

The publicity for our visit to Frunze had fallen through, and the organizers hadn't sold a single ticket, so we decided to go out into the streets ourselves and invite people to come. I was to learn what it's like to feel that you are in a zoo. Everywhere we went, people would just stop and stare at us. We went to the university, and a large crowd gathered, and I felt prompted to speak.

I stood on the stairs of one of the campus buildings and told the people that I had a message for Frunze. I said that God was the answer to their problems. About 600 people stood and listened, but I could tell by her expression that our woman promoter, who had come with us, was angry.

One piece of good news we received was that "all the musicians in the city" would be attending our concert. I guess they were intrigued to see a Western band in action. The Russian band Continua would play before us, we were informed.

The next day I visited a Baptist church and gave out Bibles and invited people from there to come to the concert. A mosque was the next place I visited. This Muslim house of worship was located in the city center. Flies buzzed around stacks of meat by the entrance.

I saw old, dark-skinned Imans (Muslim clergymen) standing outside, having a discussion. As I approached them, they stopped talking, and they gave me a look that indicated they were wondering who this strange-looking foreigner was.

"God has sent me to you," I said through our translator. They looked startled.

"He has?" one of them asked.

"Yes," I pressed on, feeling an instant empathy with them. "God wants me to give you these books." They were beautifully-produced volumes written in the local Cossack language and they told of the life of Jesus. They carefully took the books from me as if they were gold.

"Would you like to come into our mosque and pray?" one of them asked.

"I would love to," I responded. I took off my shoes, and walked into the back of the mosque. And while others were kneeling, I too knelt and asked God that Jesus would make his presence known in this mosque.

As I was preparing to leave, one of the holy men stopped me and said, "Would it be all right if our young people came to your concert tonight?" Apparently, while I was praying, our translator had explained to them who I was.

"Of course," I replied, taken aback. "They would be most welcome."

Meanwhile Keith and The Captain, our bass player, had gone to the local Muslim university. They were escorted to different classrooms and were given the opportunity to talk about the concert, but they also took the opportunity to share about Jesus. They gave out hundreds of Russian tracts and 600 students promised to attend the concert.

On the night of the show, a reporter from Russian national radio arrived and asked me for an interview. I was able to explain to the listeners about the message of Jesus and why we were there.

About 1,200 people packed the concert hall that night, including a group of uniformed Russian soldiers. During the performance, a man was standing in front of the stage with his little boy, so I leaned over and picked up the child. As I held him, I told the audience, "I have two little boys. One is five and the other eight," I said. "I care about their future. I don't want them to be sick. I want them to have a nice place to live and good food to eat because I am a good father who loves his children."

Then, lifting the boy up high so everyone could see him, I declared, "God is the same. He wants to pick you up and hold you in his arms, just like I'm holding this boy in my arms."

I called on people to come onto the stage with me if they wanted a relationship with Jesus. Eleven came forward and prayed publicly with me. While we were praying together, a man wearing a dark suit jumped on the stage and, in Russian, told the audience, that they didn't have to listen to this garbage and if they wanted to hear good music they should come to his church. I was trying to pray with these young people, but he just continued screaming at them. "When was the last time you were in church? Look at the way you are dressed. You look terrible," he yelled.

I told those on stage with me to wait for a moment and I went to this man and asked, "Can we talk for a minute?" He faced me with a cold, stern eye.

"Don't you see that these kids want to know Jesus?" I said, bursting into tears. "Why can't we just work together? Why are you doing this?"

His angry expression didn't waver even a flicker, and he just walked away, feeling he had done what was required of him.

Wiping the anguished tears from my eyes I returned to complete my prayer with the young people. Many others wanted to come as well but were afraid because of the Muslim culture. We discovered this later when several came backstage secretly to talk with us and to reveal their fears.

Meanwhile Keith was talking with eight Muslim students who were preparing to be professors at the university. Four of them also prayed to receive Christ. Later we found out that when they attempted to go to the Baptist church, they were turned away by the pastor who had taken over our microphone because he said they were from a Muslim background. So they began their own house church.

Feeling totally drained by what had occurred, we drove from Frunze to the airport in Alma-Ata, an all-day drive, and as I boarded the plane, I thought, *Finally, I can just rest, not think about anything and space out.* It was a long flight to Novosibirsk and I was feeling extremely tired. I glanced in my carry-on bag and saw a stack of Russian tracts. Then I suddenly had an unmistakable impression that we were to pass out these tracts to those on the plane.

Fortunately, I was sitting by the window, but I noticed that Keith had an aisle seat.

"Keith, take these tracts and pass them out to everybody on the plane!" I instructed him.

"No way," he hissed.

"You wimp! You big baby!" I yelled.

"You do it," Keith countered.

"I can't. I'm next to the window," I said smugly.

"No, I won't do it."

"OK," I said piously, "But just pray and ask God if you should do it."

He shrugged his shoulders with resignation. "Give me the tracts," he said in an irritated tone. He then got up and while the No Smoking sign was still on, went from the front of the plane to the back passing out copies of a Russian tract entitled, "The Road to Salvation Through Jesus."

Nobody complained, but all eagerly took the tracts. The entire plane was silent as people busily read them. A few minutes later, somebody sitting in front of me, passed me a note in English which said, "Who are you? Why are you here? Please answer!"

I scribbled a reply explaining that we were a Western band and that we loved God. I then got a note back saying that he was part of a team of Russian soccer players. The message ended, "Good luck!"

After the concert in Novosibirsk, we went on to Irkutsk, near the Mongolian border. Dead tired, we were driven through the polluted, broken-down city, to a dirty, dilapidated hotel. Our first concert was great. A Russian band called Principals of Infinity played before us and were similar in style to Talking Heads in America. The lead singer was a former physicist who had discovered that he had much more freedom to express himself if he was in a rock'n'roll band than if he stayed a scientist.

During our performance, we had a great rapport with the audience, and I threw hundreds of Bible tracts into the crowd. A local TV crew came for an interview as well as newspaper reporters, and I was able to speak directly to them about my faith in Jesus Christ. This naturally multiplied our impact in the city.

The next day I gave the promoter some Bibles and teaching materials. He said, surprisingly, that he believed we had been sent by God and he revealed that he had gone through a kind of spiritual warfare to get us there. This really struck me as an unusual comment for him to make because he was not a Christian.

At our third concert in Irkutsk, I invited people to receive Jesus into their heart and twenty-one responded publicly. At the fourth and final concert, ten people responded and prayed on stage to receive Christ.

Andrez, the drummer from the Russian band, prayed with Keith and me in our hotel room that evening to accept Jesus. Before we left the next day, Andrez said that he knew his life had changed. We challenged him to get involved in a local church.

We then moved on to Barnaul, a city formerly closed to outsiders. We were the first Western rock band to play there. In this city of 700,000 people, there were only two small evangelical churches. When we arrived I felt totally exhausted, and because the band's nerves were frazzled, we were becoming easily irritated with each other. I knew this was not a good witness and we really needed God's mercy to continue.

I didn't want to speak at our first concert. But when people started laughing at me, I decided to do it anyway. Eight people came forward to receive Christ, and some thirty followed us backstage. I did a long interview with a newspaper reporter after the concert and was asked to dedicate a baby the next day at a Russian Orthodox church.

At the second concert, we had a crazy audience. While Keith was trying to keep people off the stage, a drunken guy took a swing at him. I again asked for a public response and, while many laughed and mocked, eight people came forward. Five others also came backstage to receive Christ that evening, including some members of a local Russian punk band.

The third concert again proved difficult. I didn't feel like preaching, but I did anyway. I talked about the story of the prodigal son, and eight young people came forward.

At the last concert, however, we really felt God's presence. Even though Keith was sick, I felt he should tell his life story. As he spoke, God's Spirit came upon everyone there. Fifty-five young people came forward to receive Christ that night. The organizers asked us for Bibles and invited us back to a Siberian rock festival in October.

The Baptist pastors in this city were open to us which meant a lot after my experience in Frunze. One of them prayed for us before we left and even insisted on giving me his Russian watch as a gift. I knew this was a big sacrifice and I was really touched.

As we stood in the airport waiting to leave, Eugene, the concert organizer there, pleaded with me to "Please come back." He added, "This city is ready to receive you back." Little did we realize when he said that, that it would be in this city that God would give us a unique strategy for church planting that would prove revolutionary in the land of *the* revolution.

David praying for a sick child

ROCK ASIA

I WAS BY NOW USED TO CONTROVERSY, but this latest one was eating away at me. I needed to talk to someone whom I trusted, who knew me and also understood our situation in Amsterdam.

So, during a trip back to the States, I made a luncheon appointment to see Dr. Arthur Rouner, senior pastor of the Colonial Church of Edina in Minneapolis. For years, Arthur had been a great support to Jodi and myself and had even visited Amsterdam on several occasions to spend time with us. "What's bothering you, David?" he asked, seeing the worried expression on my face.

"I don't know what to do," I said desperately. "A lot of people whom I respect greatly, are telling me that I shouldn't go on this next tour with the band, and I understand why they feel this way, but I have such a strong conviction that I must go.

"I almost feel, Arthur, that my whole life will be a failure if I don't go on the tour."

Arthur had faced many difficult situations in his own life and so could speak out of personal experience.

"David, the way I see it," he said, "you have two choices: you can move to Fergus Falls, Minnesota, and pump gas and be a burned-out missionary, or you can risk it all.

"It may mean that you will lose everything: the band, many of your friends, everything. But the only way you'll ever do great things for God is to be willing to take risks—to live out on the edge!"

So, after lunch, I decided to go for a long walk in the woods close to his church. As I walked and listened to the constant chatter of the birds and enjoyed the beauty around me, I came to a decision. I wasn't going to move to Fergus Falls!

This was probably the weakest I'd ever felt before a tour. Coming from a busy time in the States, I had two days to "rest" in Amsterdam (which consisted of speaking, attending meetings, and practicing with the band). To add to the pressure, Russell had decided not to go on the tour, so we had to quickly train up a new guitarist, Terry Knox from Oregon.

On October 6th 1990, we flew to Moscow. When we arrived, Moscow's international airport was in absolute chaos! People were running all over the airport, fighting for a place in line or for luggage carts, which were in desperately short supply. A long line formed to get carts and after waiting almost an hour, with no movement, we decided to just grab all our stuff and push forward towards the customs barrier.

Again, we waited and waited. Then one of the band got the bright idea of just shoving all our stuff to the front. So that's what we did. To my utter amazement, we passed through security totally unchecked! This was quite remarkable when you consider we had fifteen pieces of luggage, besides all our carry-on bags.

Not sure if anyone would meet us, we bartered a taxi ride down from sixty dollars to ten dollars for a ride to a hotel boat where we had to pay a hundred dollars for a tiny, smelly double room. This was the cheapest place available to us in Moscow.

Next day we rose early and left for the domestic airport at 7:30 a.m. If we thought the international airport was chaotic, it was a place of absolute calm compared to the domestic airport. People were sleeping in doorways. There were long, tired lines of families in dirty, broken-down lobbies. The scene resembled an over-crowded, inner-city bus station in America.

We went to a separate building run by Intourist, which was provided as a special service to foreigners. This proved a real blessing because we didn't have to battle the lines in the regular terminal. After a couple of hours of waiting, a journalist sent by Eugene, the promoter, greeted us with our tickets to Barnaul where we had been invited to play in the Rock Asia festival.

Relieved that we weren't stranded, we loaded our bags into a special compartment of the plane and took our seats for our Aeroflot flight to Siberia.

The Soviet airline is not known for its perks. In fact, if your seat belt works you consider you've hit the jackpot.

After a four-hour flight from Moscow, we arrived in Barnaul to be greeted by Eugene, who appeared very pleased to see us again.

"Since your visit in April, I've only thought about your return!" he said, his eyes glistening with emotion. "We must set up a NLM fan club in Barnaul. It would be the first western program of its sort in the area!"

As Eugene said that, I wasn't very excited with the idea, but before I could say anything negative, he explained. "This would be a special fan club that would study the Bible and other Christian propaganda."

When I heard that I became excited. I let my mind run wild. The idea came to me that, after our concerts, we would tell all those who prayed to receive Jesus, "We want to start a fan club in your city." We would then introduce them to a fan club leader who could give them Bibles, T-shirts and music cassettes. These fan clubs would finally lose their fan club identity and blossom into churches.

Eugene told us that some twenty bands would participate in Rock Asia—from Japan, China, and the USSR, as well as our band from Holland.

"All the concerts are sold out and will be televised. Would you mind playing three times?" he said excitedly.

"Mind? Of course not!" I said.

Our first concert would be part of a John Lennon memorial concert. We would also be the main act on the final night, and two bands would play before us.

As we drove through the city to our hotel, the air was heavy with pollution and dust blew everywhere. A city with a population of 700,000, Barnaul is extremely run-down. Most of the side streets are just unpaved mud holes. The buildings are gray and overcrowded, while buses blow black smoke into the air.

Even though Barnaul is in the middle of a vast wilderness and forest, the air is badly polluted by heavy industry and lack of environmental controls.

Despite being completely exhausted I barely slept that night. With the thirteen-hour time change and my mind racing, I just couldn't relax.

After a brisk cold shower the next morning (because there was no hot water in the hotel), I met with some friends I had made on the previous trip. They were Pastors Victor and Nicholas from the Barnaul Baptist church, a fellowship of about 300 members. We spoke about working together to follow-up on the young people who would respond at our concerts.

The pair had brought with them Alexander, the youth pastor, and I could tell by the expression on his face that he wasn't so enthusiastic about the arrangement. He said he would give us an answer about cooperating after witnessing our first concert.

In front of the band, I acted full of faith for what lay ahead—but inside me I was emotionally and physically drained. Lying in my hotel room that evening all I could say was, "God have mercy upon us!" But after a good night's sleep—the first for some time—the next morning I felt much better. I went for a walk in the woods with Sergei, a student from a local university, who was to be our translator. As we walked and talked he told me we were close to a secret military base.

He then confided in me that he believed his country to be on the edge of revolution. As he spoke, prophetically as it turned out, I realized that this would be a window of time for the Soviet Union — God's time to break through with a new revolution of love.

Of the two bands scheduled to play before us at the John Lennon memorial concert, the first was called Principles of Infinity, who were our friends from Irkutsk. We'd had contact with them in April. During our first visit, Andre, the drummer, had prayed to receive Christ, and he agreed to be my translator when we played.

The other band was from China. Throughout their concert, they wore demonic masks. It was obviously a very religious exercise, and you could really feel the demonic atmosphere.

As we prayed before the concert, The Captain (our bass player) was sick and coughing; Terry complained of a bad stomach; and I felt sick and depressed. The only one who was feeling OK was our drummer Paul. I decided that, because it was our first concert, I wouldn't speak at the end or ask for a public response. I would just throw Bibles into the audience and say a few things between the songs.

After all, this was the John Lennon memorial concert, not a Billy Graham evangelistic meeting. We all agreed that this was the way to go.

But as we started the show I immediately felt God's heart for the people. In spite of my previous decision, I changed my mind. I wondered what John Lennon would have thought about the words that were being projected on the screen behind us. I'm sure he never would have "imagined" it!

God was powerfully in the auditorium. After explaining the message of the cross, I invited people to respond. Thirty young people worked their way towards the stage and joined me and kneeled there to ask Jesus into their lives. Many conversations about God also took place afterwards.

I then talked with the youth pastor from the Baptist church and he told me he now understood how

God was with us, and that he needed to help us reach the lost young people of Barnaul.

"We need each other!" I said as we emotionally embraced.

Finding it hard to hold back the tears, I finally fell into bed at 3:15 a.m. — but I didn't fall asleep until 6 a.m.

The next morning, we drove to a Soviet elementary school. In the lunch room, several members of the band talked to different classes and answered questions from the students. I taught them the song, "God's not dead," in English! I could see the incredible irony of this situation. Here we were in communist Siberia, singing "God's not dead," while in America this would be illegal in a public (state) school. What a crazy, mixed-up world we were living in!

Afterwards, we answered more questions from students and had a great discussion with the principal. We gave her a Russian Bible and she asked us to all sign it. "Please come back again, soon!" she said, and we told her we would try.

At the Rock Asia concert hall we had our first follow-up meeting. Three Russian boys and Pastor Victor came, and we met in a dirty closet. The boys asked good questions about the step they had taken and Rocky, who was helping the band, tried to answer their questions. Pastor Victor also explained different aspects of following Jesus. After about an hour we agreed to have another follow-up meeting on Friday.

At 1 p.m. Rocky and I then met with Eugene, the concert organizer. Eugene told me that he wanted to promote NLM nationally through TV, newspapers, and the radio. He said he understood that our purpose was to tell people about Jesus and that he was committed to making the band known throughout the Soviet Union. He also told me he would contact the local churches so we could work together with them. He went on to say that he was ready to begin the first NLM fan club which, he reiterated, would study the Bible and other "religious propaganda."

He also challenged us to continue to get involved in the schools.

"They are ready to receive you!" he added.

We talked about setting up a national tour the following year. He explained that it was essential that we had a promotional video made for this purpose. Rocky and I walked out of the meeting absolutely amazed, especially as Eugene was still an unbeliever!

Later that evening we held a concert in a youth club. In many ways it was a frustrating experience. As I threw Bibles into the crowds, many drunk guys fought over them and continually bothered those who wanted to pray with us. In the confusion I believe many were touched — but it was definitely not an easy night.

Eugene then asked me if I wanted to go with him and some others on a helicopter ride through the Altai Mountains. I gladly accepted and we left the next morning at 8:30 a.m. I was going to be traveling with Eugene, some journalists, and the former manager of Pink Floyd. It was a spectacular trip as we soared through mountain gorges and valleys.

Throughout the flight, the journalists were constantly drinking vodka, and they were all pretty "loose" when we finally landed on the side of a mountain for lunch. As I got out and the rotors continued to spin, it was comforting to see that at least the pilots were not drinking like the rest of them.

We had landed near a cabin and I walked with my translator, Sergei, to meet some people living on the mountain. I gave them a Russian Bible and my florescent yellow sunglasses. They proudly showed me their home and gave me a piece of their home-made bread to eat and a glass of fresh milk to drink.

It was now time to play again at Rock Asia. Much to my surprise we were going to be the main act at the festival—the last band to play on the last day. The Chinese band playing before us was doing a demonic ritual on stage. The singer appeared to be actually calling demons down, and apparently would become possessed by them and start to scream while the band played heavy, depressive background music.

I went back to the artists' room to pray, but felt uncomfortable because a girl was already there leading a group in some kind of Buddhist meditation, and pornographic movies were being screened on the video. I stood outside, alone in the hallway, and was overwhelmed by the spiritual pressure that I felt in this festival.

"God, speak to me," I cried out.

I turned to I Samuel 21, where I read the story of David. David needed a sword to fight with (verse 9) so he went to the priest and asked him if he had a sword for him. "The only sword I have is the one from Goliath whom you killed," the priest said.

David said, "Bring it to me, there is no other sword like it in the whole kingdom." So now, David was going to use a sword that had been used against God's people to fight on behalf of God's people.

As I read this, I felt as though God was speaking to me. He said, "A sword that has been used by Satan to destroy many people, I am now giving you." When I read this, I knew that I had nothing to fear.

The band came and joined me and we held a prayer meeting. Eventually, the stage manager came and told us it was time to go backstage and we would begin shortly.

As we were about to step out onto the stage, I suddenly felt an overwhelming feeling of anger. Throughout the four-day festival, the nineteen bands from China, Japan, and the USSR, had had a lot to say about the energy and the force of good and evil—the "god" force within us. As I was preparing for the concert, I felt God say, "Tell them I'm not a force, but a Father."

We started, but things immediately began to go wrong. First my microphone broke, so I had to take another mike from Terry, our guitarist. Then we crashed into each other and I broke a switch on his guitar. But it didn't matter. I knew that God was with us. The heavy, oppressive spirit left by the previous band could not stand up to God's great power.

As we played, the words of our songs were flashed onto the screen in Russian and I threw Bibles into the audience.

After our last song, I declared, through my Russian interpreter, "God is not a force. God is not both good and evil. God is not an energy we control. God is a Father and he has a broken heart."

I felt then God's Spirit break through into the audience. I explained about sin and how we could have a relationship with this almighty Father because he sent his son Jesus, who died and then rose again. As I spoke, someone shouted obscenities back at me, but I knew it didn't matter.

"If you need to know this Father, then come to the stage and kneel with me," I concluded.

The stage quickly filled with a steady stream of young people who joined me to receive Jesus into their hearts. As I watched them coming, the burden I had felt all week lifted dramatically off my shoulders. The heaviness left as I witnessed what God was doing that night.

It was an emotional scene at the airport the next day. Eugene told me that when we first came in April, he was a member of the Communist Party. But since then he had realized that God was the answer. He was now even closer to giving his life over to God.

"You must get into the schools," he said. "Can you and Jodi come back in January? They are ready to receive you. We need you to come back."

I told him we would try, and we waved goodbye and boarded our plane to Moscow. As our jet soared upwards through the clouds, I felt tears again sting my eyes. We had once again, in our total weakness, seen God gain the victory against all odds.

ROCK PRIEST

"JODI, IT WOULD BE GREAT if you would go with me back to Siberia," I told my wife over breakfast in our Amsterdam apartment.

"But what about the boys?" she asked. "Who'll look after them?"

I told Jodi that I was sure that one of our friends would be only too glad to take care of the boys for us while we were away on this important trip.

Once we were able to arrange for this, Jodi was happy to accompany me. But it seemed every possible barrier was put in our way to prevent us from going. Up until the last minute, our tickets were not confirmed within the Soviet Union. Our passports were kept in our office located in the city. The day before we were due to leave, I received a call at home from Michael de Jong, my right-hand man who was responsible for the new church that was planted from our work in Amsterdam.

"David, someone has broken into the office and stolen your passports," he said.

I was stunned. "Can't anything happen without a fight?" I anguished.

"I guess not," he replied sympathetically.

Jodi and I rushed to the US embassy to try to get two new passports. They were issued in record time. We then dashed over to the Soviet embassy to get our visas to go to Russia.

You never know what is going to happen when you arrive at this Embassy. There are always long lines of angry people awaiting their travel documents, but miraculously, we were able to get our visas—just seconds before they closed the office for the day. If we hadn't received them then, the whole trip would have fallen through.

When we arrived in Moscow, I was surprised by the relative quiet in the International Airport. We were told that travel to Moscow was way down because of the unrest in the country, especially in the Baltic Republics. Unlike the pandemonium I had experienced on the previous visit, the atmosphere was extremely subdued and we passed easily through customs with our suitcases stuffed full of thousands of Russian Bible tracts and other literature. I concluded the reason why we didn't have to open our suitcases was that I had Jodi with me and this made me look respectable.

After we had cleared customs, a Russian man approached us and said, "Don't I know you?" It turned out he had prayed with me to receive Christ at one of our previous concerts. He said he had received a letter from us and was quite happy to arrange a hotel for us. Like the previous time, we stayed on a hotel boat and paid $80 for a room about the size of a closet.

Misha, one of Eugene's assistants, met us the next morning at the hotel and drove us across town to the domestic airport. The freeways in Moscow are insane and we nearly crashed into a truck as the car weaved in and out of the clogged traffic.

After praying hard for two hours that we wouldn't die on the road, we arrived at the terminal which, unlike the International Airport, was full of long lines of tired and anxious people hoping to make their flight.

As we flew to Barnaul, Jodi got into a long conversation with the man sitting next to her. She explained to him why we were there and he responded by telling Jodi that what the people in the Soviet

Union needed at that time was to hear about God. "This is the right time to bring this message," he said. God was left out of his entire education, he explained, so there was a huge gap in his ability to make sense out of life.

When we arrived in Barnaul, Eugene's face broke into a huge smile as we emerged through the barrier. He extended an exuberant hand towards me which I took with an even more exuberant grip.

"We have counted the days to your arrival," he said. Our friend proceeded to hand me a schedule packed with meetings with the press, TV and local schools.

We checked in at our hotel and were happy to find it was warm (this is not always the case) as the outside temperature was minus 60 degrees Fahrenheit, but discouraged to find there was no water at all in the building. The whole section of the city where we were located was without water.

With the combination of the overpowering effects of jet lag and the pounding sound of the disco in the room next to us, we didn't get much sleep that night. Next morning we tried to freshen up as best we could with no water, and traveled to our first scheduled meeting at a Siberian prison.

The military commander led us through the arctic air to his office. The prisons in the Soviet Union are run by the military and make Western prisons look like holiday camps. The wind clawed at my face as he led us through the courtyard, where icicles hung from the surrounding roofs. We were puffing white vapor as we breathed in the frozen air.

We entered a room where I was told I could address the prisoners. I noticed that all the men had their heads shaved and wore old, tattered clothes.

A drum was beating incessantly and prisoners were marching between the buildings in time with the beat.

As Jodi and I came into the room, the men stood at attention. The commander then gave them permission to be seated and told me stiffly that I could now address the men. I noticed that none of them dared look at Jodi. They had probably been warned not to, and I thought they would probably be harshly treated if they ever stepped out of line.

"I want to tell you about somebody who suffered the death sentence," I began, as the wind outside began to gust up, throwing snow against the windows. The men watched me curiously as I continued.

"In America," I said, "you are sent to prison to be punished for a crime, and when it's real serious you get the death sentence—often the electric chair." Many of the men gave me more attention when they heard that.

"I want to tell you about somebody who wasn't guilty of anything, yet he received the death sentence. In fact, he died for the bad things we did," I explained.

I told them about Jesus Christ and how he died for us on a cross because God wanted to have a personal relationship with us and wanted to forgive us of our guilt.

"If any of you men need to know God and receive Jesus Christ into your heart, I want to invite you to come to the front and kneel with me," I said.

The commander gave permission for this, and about ten men worked their way to the front and we knelt together.

After we had prayed, some of the prisoners stayed behind and asked questions and Jodi and I gave those who responded Bibles and other tracts. The others silently filed out and returned to their cells.

Later we had tea with the commander and other military officers from the prison.

Next morning there was a knock on the door of our hotel room. It was the head of the local Foreign Language Institute. We had a long talk with this lady about God and also pride. She was a well-educated woman, fluent in many languages and held a prestigious position in the community. I told her that if she wanted to know God she needed to humble herself and get rid of all the pride she had in her heart. To my surprise she agreed and asked if we could talk again at another date.

Our next meeting was at a nearby high school. There was an article in a local paper about our time at the prison the day before, and the reporter had referred to me as the "Rock Priest." It was a positive article and the students in the school were very excited to meet this Rock Priest, from America.

Before we had left for this trip, the band had made three twenty-minute videos of No Longer Music and our messages about God. We now showed one of them to the students and answered the many questions they had. Jodi was constantly surrounded by groups of young people who wanted her to sign their booklets and she would write long notes of dedication in each one.

A TV crew came to the school and we gave them an interview about our upcoming LP, *No Sex* (before marriage). They thought the title was hilarious. They asked many questions about it and about my faith in God. I couldn't believe that this was all taking place in the heart of Siberia.

The next day was a little warmer—the temperature shot up to minus 40 degrees Fahrenheit. We visited a Junior College, and as I addressed the students (something I would not be allowed to do in America!) I told them that the world was no accident, and that God had made the beautiful mountains. He wasn't a force or energy, but a Father with a broken heart who loved them and wanted to give them hope and a new life.

A teacher raised her hand and asked a question. "You seem to be sharing this from deep inside yourself," she said. "And for that you must have suffered to bring this message."

I explained that it was true that I had pain in my heart, but that it was not because I had suffered. "The reason for this pain," I said, "is because most of you don't know God's great love for you. That makes me extremely sad." Suddenly, without warning, I began to cry. It was as though God's presence came into that silent lecture room, and throughout the room, many others were also in tears.

I felt God didn't want me to invite people to come forward and receive Jesus right then, but rather to let them respond individually.

We gave everyone booklets and explained how they could know Jesus, and we had some deep conversations afterwards, including one with the principal of the school.

Jodi and I then traveled to a school where I had been the previous year. It was for exceptional students between the ages of fifteen and eighteen. Many of them had made decisions for God during the Rock Asia festival and had attended follow-up Bible studies at the festival. These students told me they read the Bible all the time and talked about God often. We showed them the video we had made, and they laughed hysterically because the Russian translation we had put on in Holland was so bad. They offered to put a more accurate translation on it before it was broadcast on Russian TV.

One of the students told me that part of my translation into Russian was totally wrong. I was saying that God is reaching out his arms, ready to forgive anyone who will come to him, but it was translated that God is waiting to decide whom he will forgive and not forgive.

From there, we traveled to the Foreign Language Institute. Most of the students in the class were in their twenties, and I spoke about the emptiness of materialism. For many of them, materialism has become the answer to all problems, so I told them of the despair and loneliness in Holland—a relatively wealthy country.

"Even rich young people are not satisfied; because the answer is not in things, but in spiritual renewal," I said.

That evening we went to Eugene's flat and made plans for an incredible tour that would begin in Moscow and end in Mongolia.

On the Sunday, after a typically life-threatening taxi ride through the city, we arrived at one of only two evangelical churches in Barnaul. It was a Baptist church with about 300 members.

Pastor Victor was there to greet us and he led us into a room where the elders were meeting. I could tell that not all the men there were thrilled with my presence, and I was a little surprised that they even allowed me to speak.

The service was held in a beautiful but unheated sanctuary. On the ground floor were mostly old women with scarves wrapped round their heads, and in the balcony a few students from the school we had visited the day before sat shivering.

On the stage sat the few men who were in the service, with the head pastor behind a table.

Throughout the proceedings, people were passing notes to the pastor. They were questions. As I waited for my time to speak, I felt increasingly nervous, wondering how I would address such an audience, especially when I knew that they were wondering about me and my appearance—I was probably the first long-haired preacher they'd ever had in their pulpit.

I was given the signal by the pastor that it was my time and walked to the pulpit with my non-Christian translator. I spoke about the lost sheep in Luke 15 and said that God was more concerned for the one lost sheep than for the ninety-nine that were not lost. He would go and find the lost sheep and not expect them to come to him.

At the conclusion of my message I asked people to kneel with me on the platform if God had spoken to their hearts, and I also said that they needed to be willing to go to the lost sheep of Barnaul.

I knelt, and many joined me weeping and praying aloud for the courage to obey God. We had a wonderful time together. After that, all their doubts about working with us disappeared and they said they really wanted us to support each other.

After we had prayed together the pastor asked me if I would sing. I thought this was a crazy idea. What could I sing to such an audience? My mind raced to some of the songs I used to sing on the bridge in Amsterdam and the only one I could think of was "Holy, Holy, Holy, Lord, God of power and might."

I asked the pastor how the lady organist would be able to accompany me if she didn't know the song.

"Don't worry about it," he beamed. "She'll just follow along as you sing."

So I again went to the front and sang the song while this woman tried to follow me on the organ. My singing was terrible, and as I sat down Jodi told me that I was totally out of tune. I felt very stupid and I knew that Jodi was trying not to be embarrassed. But then Pastor Victor told me how much they loved my singing!

That evening Jodi and I went to Natasha's apartment. She and her husband were directors in the local university, but their apartment was so cold we all had to wear jackets. When I was there before, they asked if I could bring back some English tapes for their students to study English. I was told that all the tapes they had were old-fashioned and didn't use up-to-date English words. So Jodi and I gave them a New International Version of the Bible on cassette to teach their students how to speak English. They said it was the most precious gift they had ever received and they immediately began to listen to the tapes.

It was finally time for Jodi and me to bid farewell to our many friends in Barnaul. Already the Moscow to Mongolia *No Sex* tour was beginning to take shape...

THE NO SEX TOUR

I STOOD ON STAGE BEFORE THE CROWD IN A MOSCOW THEATER AND YAWNED. "I'm tired," I sighed, stretching my arms in the air. "Where's my bed?" Cheers broke out as a bed on wheels was pushed out onto the stage, resplendent with tailpipes, flashing lights, sirens and prohibited road signs.

I then put a long, striped nightgown over my stage clothes and stood on top of the red, satin-sheeted bed.

"I believe in sex," I yelled to the crowd. They cheered wildly in response.

"I believe you should have sex as often as possible," I continued, as they cheered even more wildly. By now these Muscovites were really worked up and enjoying every moment of my performance.

So I hit them really hard. "After marriage, of course!"

They suddenly became quiet. While being pushed around in the bed I sang our song, as the words were projected on a screen in Russian:

This song's for all of you practicing safe sex,
Thinking AIDS is the worst thing you can get.
What will keep you safe from emotions that are
wrecked?
The only lasting sex you'll have will be with a
video cassette.
No sex before marriage, no sex.

This song's for all of you laying in your bed,
Staring at the ceiling wishing you were dead.
The only lasting lover is the pillow in your bed;
You run around like a chicken that's lost its
head.
No sex before marriage, no sex.

God sees the unwed mothers,
The lonely lives,
And all the others:

Aborted babies, the world's insane.
Jesus cries when he sees all the pain.
No sex before marriage, no sex.

The message hit home!

We had been on the road now for just four days. In spite of many delays and difficulties in Moscow, where we had performed twice, we were in good spirits. The concerts there were poorly planned and promoted, but in spite of this, thirty-five young people came to Christ and were followed up by a Moscow evangelistic church.

Eugene, our concert organizer, had arranged for us to have a private jet and we went to the airport to see it for the first time. He had made the arrangements because of the great distances we would be traveling on this, our longest tour yet. It would have been nearly impossible to have made it overland without extending the tour for months.

Our international touring team consisted of fourteen people and thousands of Bibles, tracts, follow-up literature and musical equipment.

This was the No Longer Music "Moscow to Mongolia" *No Sex* tour.

Traveling ahead of us were special intercession teams who were to pray for us in each of the cities in which we were to perform. Part of the strategy was that in each city a team of fan club leaders (who were really church planters), would stay behind to help nurture those who would respond.

Originally Eugene had promised two planes, and we became concerned when he only produced one aircraft to transport the team and all the equipment and literature.

After arriving at the airfield, prepared to fly to Tashkent, the capital of Uzbekistan, we discovered that our plane was a very small, three-engine aircraft with no cargo hold. The only way we could get all our stuff into the plane was by removing the door and taking out half the seats.

We piled equipment in the toilet area from the floor to the ceiling. There were no straps to hold the cargo in place, so if we hit any turbulence, the huge flight cases could come crashing down upon us. The only way to get into the plane our selves was by climbing up a ladder on the wing and crawling through a small window.

Some members of our group, fearing the worst, began to say that we would be overweight and might crash. People panicked, with visions that what happened to Keith Green, would also happen to us. (His small plane crashed in Texas after being over-loaded.)

Victor, our sound engineer, took out a flashlight and began examining the wings for cracks.

"Maybe we shouldn't go on the trip," said one of the team members. But it was no wonder we were experiencing a spiritual conflict — we were going to Tashkent, a closed Islamic stronghold in Soviet Central Asia.

To try and relieve the tension, I said firmly, "Soviet pilots are the best trained in the world." I wasn't sure if this was true, but I said it anyway.

"But we're overweight," one of the members of the team wailed.

It was difficult for me at this point not to get extremely angry. But I said, "OK, let's figure out how much everything weighs." So Victor began calculating the weight of all the equipment and then asked everyone for their personal weight.

When Terry Knox, our guitarist, told Victor his weight one of the band members shouted out, "No way, Terry, you weigh more than that!"

Everyone was extremely tense. Victor and I climbed back out through the window to the pilot, who had previously been a MIG fighter-pilot, and we showed him the estimated weight. I said, "Do you think she can fly with all this weight?"

"No problem," he said.

I estimated we were well overweight, but his reassuring words were good enough for me. As I relayed the news to the rest of the team, they reluctantly got back into the plane through the window—and began a prayer meeting.

The aircraft was a strange sight. There were people sitting on one side and on the other, flight cases and boxes were stacked up to the ceiling.

The pilot started up the engines and headed down the runway. As we began racing forward, all of us began to pray that we would actually get off the ground. Suddenly, Gerritt Ensing, our band pastor, started running up and down the aisles, praying wildly.

"Sit down, Gerritt," I said. "Put your seat belt on."

I managed to get him back in his seat. I thought about my family and concluded that God wouldn't let us crash. There was too much important work ahead for us.

Rick Adams, our special-effects specialist from New York, wanted to sit by me because, as he said, "If we are going to die, I want to be by you."

As we surged into the air, you could feel a collective sigh of relief from the group. Our next crisis was during the landing. I shut my eyes and waited for the moment when the wheels struck the ground. The plane screamed along the Tashkent runway as it braked, and we all breathed a little easier at the wonderful moment of safe landing.

After three-and-a-half hours of sleep in a cockroach-infested hotel, I was in prayer, asking God what sort of approach I should take in the concert that night. In the hotel lobby, I saw an ominous picture of what looked to me like Iran's Ayatollah Khomeini.

From the window of our hotel, I could see a giant mosque where a large Islamic convention was taking place.

Tashkent, which was at that time the fourth largest city in the Soviet Union with nearly two million people, bordered Iran and Afghanistan, and the people were said to be very aggressive towards Christianity.

The city council had just passed a law making it illegal to preach the gospel. The week we were there, the Iranians had also issued a decree in Teheran, that to kill all Americans everywhere was a holy, Islamic duty.

Victor had come to me that day with an article he had read in *USA Today,* warning Americans not to go to this region of the world. However, I still felt we needed to be bold, and I knew that we should not be intimidated by all the threats.

The first concert was great. We played with a non-Christian band called 09, and while we were on stage I could feel the power of God. I didn't ask people to respond publicly, although I knew if I had, many would have done so. I was warned about this by Eugene. He told me that somebody had been there recently with the Jesus film and a riot had broken out after it had been screened.

I ended the second concert by saying, "I know people in Uzbekistan love their children. What we have seen up on the stage is a love story about the great God and his creation."

It was my plan to stop there, but I just couldn't help myself and so I went on to explain who Jesus was, and eight people came forward to receive God. I was then told by Eugene that there were people in attendance from the local government who would decide if we would be able to do any more concerts.

I was afraid that after what I had just done they would cancel the rest of our concerts.

The next day I met with two people from the only Baptist church in Tashkent. They told me that they were under a lot of pressure because of the laws forbidding evangelization in the city.

I could sense a deep fear in the city and it seemed that people on the street were very tense. Still the authorities allowed us to proceed, and while we were setting up for the concert that afternoon, I did a television interview. I explained that our concert was about a Father's love for his children and said that everybody needed to experience that love.

"How's it going?" I asked the singer from the band 09. He explained that he was feeling sick to his stomach. I felt compelled to pray for him that God would heal him and so I asked him, "Would it be OK if I prayed for you and ask God to make your stomach feel better?" He agreed, and afterwards said he felt much better.

Many more people were at the concert. While we were playing our second song, "I Want To Praise You Lord," I jumped off the drum stage, lost my balance and landed heavily on my left heel.

My body twisted round as a searing pain shot through my leg and I almost fainted. My legs felt suddenly horribly unsteady, the muscles trembling and untrustworthy, but somehow I was able to complete the concert. In great agony and with my face pale, I was somehow able to invite those that were there to receive Jesus into their hearts. Six people publicly responded.

A journalist, there to do a story, broke down in tears when she tried to interview me. She was so touched by the message that she had heard.

By now I could hardly think straight because of the pain. My head ached and the muscles of my legs felt completely out of joint. Somehow I had to make it through the next concert, and so Karen, who was the tour nurse, tried to strap my ankle. My face was grim with pain, but I somehow made it through. Twenty three people responded after the concert, and I was then carried to an old ambulance which transported me to a primitive hospital where my leg was X-rayed. My foot was by now very swollen, and I knew that doing two more concerts on it wouldn't help matters.

The white-coated doctor, after putting my leg in a cast, told me through a translator, "I'm afraid you won't be able to walk on this for three weeks."

"Why?" I asked, with a sick, sinking feeling in my stomach.

"Well, you haven't broken it, but you have sustained severely torn ligaments," he said gravely.

After being released from the hospital at about 1:30 a.m., I was carried to my hotel room. I was extremely tired and discouraged. The last thing I remember before dropping off to sleep was asking desperately, "Why doesn't God heal my ankle?"

The next morning a depressed looking Eugene knocked at the door. "David, we need to cancel the rest of the concerts here," he said glumly. "You need to rest."

"I'm sorry, Eugene," I replied as firmly as I could. "I appreciate your concern for me, but we can't do that. Anyway, I am feeling a lot better." Actually, I felt like death warmed over, but I wanted to keep him from halting the tour. I was determined to do the concerts, even if I had to do them from a bed.

Later that afternoon, I developed a bad case of diarrhea and that added to my gloom. Jeff Gott, our tour manager, gave me some medicine for it. It stopped the problem, but I still felt terrible.

A wild-looking cab driver came to my room to take me to the concert hall. He carried me on his back from the cab to the back-stage area. He told me that he had received Christ the day before at one of our concerts and said he was glad I was in his city.

Several things were on my mind when I entered the concert hall. First, I was desperately hoping that I wouldn't get sick on stage from all the medicine I had in me. Second, I was wondering how the concert would go because we had to cancel a lot of the stage show, including the powerful presentation of the gospel through a drama that we performed with live music.

The curtain was closed but I could hear the crowd on the other side. Someone carried me to a flight case and I sat there in front of the curtain.

"I can't believe I'm doing this," I shouted to the band members.

Suddenly, the curtain opened and we started the concert. I grasped the cordless radio mike and wheeled myself around on the flight case. One of the songs was supposed to end with me jumping up and down three times. I managed to get off the flight case and hop up and down three times, but on the third hop I fell over and had to crawl on my hands and knees back to the flight case. I must have been a pathetic sight.

I thought that I might as well say something so very simply I explained the message of the cross. What happened after that was amazing. I felt a tremendous sense of God's power and young people literally began to run forward to the stage to receive Christ.

More people came to Jesus that night when I was sick and unable to walk, than when I was well and we were able to do our "powerful" drama.

Igor, from 09, was close to tears as we prepared to leave. We gave the names and addresses of 154 new Christians to the Baptist church, who were planning to visit all those who had responded.

I went back to the hotel, still sick, and again had to be carried to my room.

After arriving in Barnaul, Siberia, I didn't sleep the entire night, and still had a bad case of diarrhea. We had flown there the previous day. I met with the support team who were planting the new church comprised of previous fan club members. They told me that a problem they were facing was that so many people were coming to Jesus that they didn't know how to follow-up on all of them.

Sitting alone in my room, waiting for a ride to the concert hall, I could see through the window the tiny Russian cars, tractors and smoke-belching buses and trucks, fighting through an unmarked intersection. Shabbily-dressed people darted across the street whenever they saw an opening.

"Jesus," I cried out, "please help me to see these poor people through your eyes."

He did. And again that night, as I sat on the flight case, some eighty people gave their hearts to Jesus.

From Barnaul we then flew to Novosibirsk. It was a large, crazy audience, but Rocky prayed for my leg and I found I could then stand on it. After the concert, thirty-eight people responded.

It seemed like things were starting to take a turn for the better, until we found out that our translator, Tayna, had just heard that her father had died. Rocky went back with her to Barnaul to attend the funeral. It was quite a shock for all of us.

From there we flew to Krasnoyarsk. I was greatly encouraged because now I could take the cast off my leg. And I even found myself in a hotel room that had hot water!

We saw 255 people come to Christ in this Siberian city, including a woman who was delivered from spiritism and left the stage literally dancing with joy.

From there we went to Irkutsk. I met with Serge who had arranged our last concert there. He had made a decision for Christ last time I was there but had fallen back into drinking vodka after his wife had left him and was completely back into "the scene."

The hotel we were using in Irkutsk was better than the one we used the last time we were there. The water was still brown, but at least it was warm. I was now really missing Jodi and the boys. It brought me lots of joy to receive a telex that arrived at the hotel, saying that Jodi would be able to meet me in Ulan Ude.

A large rowdy crowd came to the concert in Irkutsk. Standing in the front were a group of Satanists who were screaming and cursing. During the concert, they took tracts that we had given to the audience and made little bonfires with them.

When Terry, our guitarist walked by them, they tried to kick him as they screamed and mocked.

Forty-two kids came on the stage to receive Christ that night, while one of the Satanists jumped onto the stage and started urinating off it, and another screamed obscenities into the microphone.

I thought to myself, *This is real spiritual warfare.*

In spite of all the distractions, seventy-two found Christ in Irkutsk over those two nights.

From there we flew to Ulan Ude, the center of Buddhism in Soviet Central Asia. I could feel a different spiritual climate as we entered the city. The band that played before us was extremely aggressive and unfriendly towards us.

I went back to the hotel before the concert and was told that two American girls had arrived and that Jodi was one of them. I ran up the stairs and opened the door and there she was with Henriette, the Dutch fiancee of Terry, the guitarist. When I saw my beautiful wife standing there, I threw my arms around her and burst into tears. It was so good to see her.

Twenty-five people came to Jesus after the concert and were followed-up by our fan club teams.

We were asked if we would like to visit the only Buddhist monastery in Soviet Central Asia. I had been told in Holland to be very careful when I visited a monastery.

"I know people who have gone to a Buddhist monastery and it has taken them days to recover," I was warned. "This is not something you should do for sightseeing. These are demonic spiritual strongholds."

I took their advice seriously and was almost paranoid when we went to the monastery. As we entered the gates, with my hand grasping Jodi's tightly, I kept looking over my shoulder to make sure that no demons were following us.

We were led into a temple that was full of different idols and other religious objects, and I saw a Buddhist monk in a saffron robe sitting at a table.

I was glad when the time came for us to leave and get back on the bus, and relieved to note that I hadn't suffered any damage from the visit.

But suddenly I felt a strong impression that God was saying, "David, I want you to go back to that monastery and give a Bible to that monk."

I thought to myself, *That's just me. That's not God.* And I ignored the thought.

But the impression came back even stronger. "I want you to give a Bible to that Buddhist monk."

So I told Jodi to wait in the bus, and asked the translator to return with me to the monastery. We walked through the gates and headed directly for the temple where I found the monk still sitting behind his desk.

"God is very pleased with you," I told him through my translator.

He stared at me with a puzzled expression.

"God is so glad that you want to know him and are seeking him," I continued. "It makes him so happy that you want to know who he is. And he is really pleased with you."

I could tell that he was extremely humbled and embarrassed by my words.

"That's why I want to give you this book," I said. "It's the Bible. And I believe this book will help you in your search for God."

He took the Bible from me and asked me if I would sign it for him. Even in the midst of a Buddhist temple, I could feel the powerful presence of the Holy Spirit.

It was four in the morning and still dark when we boarded a cold bus for the train station. Hordes of people were there, all shouting and fighting their way onto the train.

After mass confusion and lots of pushing and shoving we managed to get on board. Each wagon was heated by a coal burning fire. After traveling all day, we had to wait nearly eight hours at the Mongolian border. A border official then asked to speak with our manager, Jeff Gott.

"There is no way you can take this equipment into our country," he said.

Jeff began to protest, when he was interrupted by the official.

"There is no baggage car on the train," the man shouted. "You have to go back."

Jeff, not being the kind of person who can take no for an answer, went to six other Mongolian officials who also said no. Just before the train was ready to cross the border a military officer accepted a Bible from us and arranged for a baggage car to be added to our train.

So, miraculously, the Mongolia tour was saved from cancellation. The cubicles in the train were unbelievably dirty and the ancient train moved extremely slowly, stopping often in the middle of nowhere. As we looked out of the window, I saw people living in tents, and men on horseback, and I wondered what in the world we were doing in Mongolia.

"These people are going to think we are from Mars," I told Jodi.

She laughed. "Sometimes I think you are from Mars!"

It was twenty-six back-breaking hours after crossing the border that we finally arrived in Ulan Bator, the capital city. At that time, there were only 100 known Christians in the entire country. All of them had been believers for only a year or less. We were to discover that this atheistic country of two million is one of the least evangelized on earth.

Our translator was Altaa, the first known Mongolian Christian in the last 800 years. English-born John Gibbens, who was married to Altaa, had recently completed the first translation of the New Testament in the primary language of the Mongolian People's Republic (also known as Outer Mongolia). He had begun the translation project some twenty years before. Mongolian is probably the last official national language in the world to receive the New Testament. John Gibbens worked side by side with Altaa to complete the work.

John is probably the foremost Western expert on Mongolia today. From him we learned that Mongolia was, up until 1921, part of China, and then became the first Socialist republic after the USSR to adopt atheism as part of the official Marxist Leninist ideology and, in 1924, prohibited all religious activities, and forced Christian missionaries out of the country.

I asked him an important question. "John, do you think it makes any sense for a band like ours to be here?"

John, whom I jokingly called "The Mad Scientist" because of the way his hair looked and his unusual manner, surprised me with his answer.

"I can't think of a more appropriate way of evangelizing Mongolia than with your band," he said. "The sons and daughters of Ghenghis Khan respond to loud noise, strength and wildness more than anything else. This is the way to do it."

I had to agree with that. We were certainly noisy and wild!

We were also told that there was no Russian-speaking church in Mongolia. Mongolia is considered one of the most violent countries in the world. It is said to have the highest rate of crimes against children. Rape is considered only natural and is rarely prosecuted. Westerners are mostly despised, which was quite the opposite of Siberia, while Russians are hated with a passion. In fact, Eugene, our Russian organizer and the others who worked with him, had to hide their identities while they were there so they wouldn't be attacked.

Because of all this, we had to be extremely careful and were told never to go out at night. Jodi and I were on our way to the concert hall after eating dinner when, behind us, a group of Mongolian guys came up and started to scream into my face. One was about to strike me when I realized that they probably thought that I was a Russian. So exaggerating my American accent, I said, "I am American. American! Rock concert. Rock and roll."

When they finally understood that we weren't Russians, they laughed and everything was fine.

The hotel we stayed in cost five cents a night. And for an additional four cents you could eat your meals there as well. Although this hotel too was full of cockroaches, at least it had hot water.

Our first four concerts were for the Russian people living there (Mongolia had been a Soviet satellite state), and in Ulan Bator, we saw 34 Russians pray to receive Christ. Entire Russian families would come forward after our concerts and we held follow-up meetings for them in a gymnasium.

As the days passed I was getting more and more physically run down. I discovered a boil on my waist, and I seemed always to have diarrhea. Jodi was never sick at all.

It was now the time for us to do our first major concert for the Mongolian people. The Philharmonic Hall was packed with about 1,000 people. After the concert was finished, I started to speak. I talked as I had been accustomed to in Siberia, about how God was a father, how he wanted to comfort those that were there and how this father God wanted a relationship with them. But the extremely hostile crowd didn't seem to respond to my message.

Only three people came to the front while others jeered and mocked. I was told later that they were making obscene jokes about those who had come forward. People were afraid to respond as they knew there was the possibility they would be beaten up afterwards. This made me feel discouraged. I thought we were going to see a great harvest in Mongolia and I didn't expect this kind of negative reaction.

The next day, Jeff and I met with John Gibbens and Altaa.

Coming straight to the point John said, "David, you've got a lot to learn." He then told me that the way I was explaining the gospel was inappropriate for the culture. "People in this country refer to God as the 'supreme intelligence' and you need to use this expression when you say who God is.

"They will not be reached if you talk about fatherhood. They're not moved by this. Instead you need to explain to them how we've lost contact with the supreme intelligence, how this supreme intelligence is Spirit but that this supreme intelligence sent his son to be a man in the flesh."

I thought about what I had learned about communicating in the symbols of the people I was trying to reach. I had vainly assumed that what had reached people in Siberia, would also have the same effect on people in Mongolia.

It was our second concert in the Philharmonic Hall. The concert was finished and after the discussions with John, I was now going to explain the gospel the way he told me to.

I sat down on the edge of the stage and said, "I would like you to meet my wife, Jodi."

Jodi then appeared on the stage, carrying a lighted candle. She sat down beside me and handed me the candle. As I held it I said, "We have two little boys, Aaron and Benjamin. What is the meaning of their lives? Do they have any more value than the flame on this candle?"

I then blew out the candle and handed it back to my wife.

"There is a supreme intelligence and I studied philosophy at university in America to try and understand who this supreme intelligence is."

(I had been told by John Gibbens that people there put a high value on education, and that is why I told them this.)

"Many of my friends in the university gave up trying to find out who this supreme intelligence is and they tried to fill their emptiness with other things—alcohol, music, sex or even more education.

"I want you to know that the supreme intelligence is a Spirit, is invisible, but sent his son Jesus as a man to show us who he is."

I explained, in their symbols, the message of the cross and how through it there was hope for them to see the supreme intelligence.

"The concert is over," I concluded. "I would like everyone to leave. But I invite anyone who wants to know this supreme intelligence to stay and we will pray together. Only those who want to know this supreme intelligence and who wish to give their lives to Jesus should stay behind. Everyone else should go."

Over 100 stayed to receive Bibles and to pray with us.

It was time for Jodi to take the train back to Siberia so she could catch her flight back to Moscow and then on to Amsterdam. I really hated to see her go, but I was glad she would be returning to the boys.

Terry and I went with Henriette and Jodi to the train station. I was told by Eugene that there would be an escort to take the girls on the train back to Ulan Ude.

As we boarded the train and they found their compartment, I felt a little uncomfortable as I saw the car-load of men who were checking out the two women. It appeared that Eugene hadn't been able to find the promised escort for them. In the compartment where they would be sleeping was a drunk guy who kept eyeing them. A Russian came on board and so Eugene asked him to watch them.

"Sure," he said, "I'll be glad to watch them."

It was then I realized that if I let them go on that train, I'd probably never see them again. So I said, "Come with me. There is no way I'm going to let you go on this train. Get your bags and let's go!"

Eugene was very upset with me and tried to explain that if they didn't go on this train, they would miss the flight and he didn't know of any way to get them back to Moscow. I told him that I didn't care.

"There is no way I am going to let them go alone on this train," I said.

Eugene felt like I didn't trust him and was hurt because of the incident, but later we were able to talk about it and resolve our differences. In the end I purchased air tickets for the two girls and flew them out of Ulan Bator to Moscow, but at least they arrived back in Holland in one piece.

It was a rough and wild four-hour ride to Dachran. In the four-wheel drive "moon vehicle" we passed burned out buses, the carcasses of half-rotted horses, and people living in tents, as well as large herds of sheep.

I was told by John Gibbens that there were only three Christians in Dachran. Our first concert was for Mongolians and about 600 attended. At the end of the performance, I again said, "I only want people to stay who want to know the supreme intelligence, who want to know Jesus." No one left.

"You don't understand," I said. "The concert is over. I only want you to stay if you want to know the supreme intelligence; if you want to know Jesus."

I was able to persuade 100 people to leave the auditorium and 500 stayed and prayed with me. John took down the names and addresses of those who responded so he could follow them up.

We traveled back to Ulan Bator and had a further concert for the Russian military garrison there.

There 125 people prayed after the concert to receive Jesus and we received a letter from a Major General in the Soviet Armed Forces commending our band. I learned we were the first foreign band ever to receive such an honor.

Eugene came to my room the next day. His hand was bandaged and it looked as though he had been crying. He told me that he had been walking to meet with someone when two Mongolian guys attacked him. He was shaken up and asked for prayer.

That same day Jeff Gott, our manager, also had a taste of life in Ulan Bator. He was in a store and his bag containing a lot of Mongolian money and personal things was stolen.

It took us two nights on the train to get back to Siberia. Black marketers set up shop in the train and the Russian train steward had two black eyes from a fight he was in with some Mongolian passengers.

After five days' traveling, we finally arrived back in Amsterdam. As a result of our tour, 1,700 people prayed with us after the concerts to know more about God and many of them made a decision afterwards to follow Jesus. New churches were started in Barnaul, Krasnoyarsk, Ulan-Ude and Novosibirsk through Operation Impact, a follow up organization that was created as a result of the *No Sex* tour.

Before we left Mongolia, John Gibbens had met with me. "David, I need workers," he said. "I will supply you with Mongolian Christians if you can send me workers. Together as a team they can go to cities in Mongolia where no church has ever existed and they could be part of history and be the first ones to plant churches where none have existed before!"

That challenge is still with me today!

My name is Max. I am now 21 years old and it was about 4 years ago that I went to the No Longer Music concert in Novosibirsk, Siberia.

At that time I went to every rock concert in the city and this Western music group really attracted my attention. So a few of my friends and I went for it!! We were all pretty wild then. My hair was long, covering my face, and I was dressed like a Heavy Metaller — old torn jeans, etc.

I really liked the music and the show itself was great. It really spoke to me and although I didn't give my life to Jesus on that night, I wanted to know more about all that stuff that David had talked about. So I wrote down my address and tele-

phone number for the Fan Club that they were going to organize.

I was then invited to a meeting and started to attend the Bible study group. It was organized by the team that came to follow up on the people from the No Longer Music concerts and soon after that I gave my life to Jesus.

I'm very thankful to God for being so patient with me and so wise in using music to present the gospel to me. I am also very thankful to David and No Longer Music for being obedient to Him and coming to Siberia to bring the good news.

The fan club has now become World of Life Church and God is still continuing with the work He started through the No Longer Music concert in Novosibirsk. I now lead one of the home groups in the church and also our worship team. Other than that I am working on my master degree as an electrical engineer. I still love music but much more than that, I love Jesus as my Lord and Savior. God bless you all and I would really like to see No Longer Music in Siberia again.

Max

Tashkent, where David hurt his leg

A calmer moment in the air over Tashkent

18
GOOD MORNING, VIETNAM

FOR A LONG TIME, I FELT THAT GOD WANTED US TO GO TO VIETNAM. So I went to Vietnam with Jeff Gott to determine if it would be possible for us to come and do a tour of the country. We were there for a week trying to make contact with city officials and plan a friendship tour. At that time, no other western band had received permission to go to Vietnam. It was still very closed to Western influences, but I felt that God wanted us there.

After four days of being turned down and being told it was impossible by government officials, we finally made contact with one of the directors of VinaConcert, a government-approved promotional agency.

They said that they wanted us to come and would set up a "Friendship Tour" for the following year. This was going to be a historic breakthrough; to be able to do a tour as a Western band in Vietnam was significant enough, not to mention the fact that we were a Christian band.

So after a year of preparation and plans, we were ready to travel to Vietnam in April 1994. There were people coming from three continents to help support the band in this effort.

Just two weeks before we were ready to leave, I received a phone call from Rocky in the Netherlands. I could tell by his tone of voice that something terrible had happened. "I've got some bad news, David." he said.

"What's that?" I asked reluctantly, not wanting to know.

"I received a fax from VinaConcert and they have canceled our tour," he replied.

I was stunned. I felt like someone had just punched me in the stomach. "Rocky, we need to fight this. I think we still need to go and I don't think we should give up," I responded, but not really believing the words I was saying.

"I'm going to go pray about this and I'll call you back in a few hours," I said as I hung up the phone.

Stunned, I went for a walk with Jodi unable to even pray. "What are we going to do, Jodi?" I said. "I can't believe this has happened after all the money and time we have invested. There are people coming from all over the world."

Jodi said, "Well, we need to ask God what to do." I was too devastated to pray myself, so she prayed and I listened. After she prayed she told me she felt that we were supposed to ask a couple of other people we were working with to pray as well. If everyone felt the same thing, we would know what God wanted us to do. So I made a few long-distance phone calls and asked others to pray. The response I got back was the same from all of them. We were supposed to go to Vietnam, even though we didn't have permission to do the concerts, and God would miraculously open the door.

So with no governmental permission to do the concerts and with a great deal of anxiety, we traveled with our band to Ho Chi Minh City. Eugene, who organized the Moscow to Mongolia No Sex tour, flew to Hanoi from Siberia a week before we arrived to help Rocky with negotiations with governmental officials.

I was anxious to get through customs so that Rocky could assure me that everything was OK and that he and Eugene had received permission for the concert tour to go ahead. But instead Rocky told me that there was no way the government was going to give us permission to do the friendship tour. He also informed me that the government had impounded all of our equipment and would not release it to us from customs. To make things even worse, Eugene had slipped on some ice in Siberia before he came and was in so much pain that he had returned home without seeing me.

I thought to myself, "That's great, here I am in Vietnam, people have come here from all over the world, we can't get our equipment from customs, we don't have permission from the government. What are we going to do?" I did everything I could to put on a brave front to the band, but inside I felt completely empty and overwhelmed by the circumstances we were in.

Rocky had arranged for us to stay in a broken down hotel which he described as "Saigon grunge." We got in a van and wove our way through the chaotic city to the hotel, exhausted from our trip. Even though I hadn't slept for about 24 hours, it was impossible for me to think about sleep. I told the band to relax, and Rocky and I had a meeting about what we were going to do.

Rocky was clearly discouraged and at the end of himself, and I couldn't blame him. He said he had tried everything he could think of and that every official that he had talked to was negative. He had completely run out of ideas. The circumstances were completely out of our control so we could do nothing except pray.

We started a 24-hour prayer chain that lasted three days. Ton and I were on the graveyard shift during this prayer time and when Ton was praying, he heard something in his bathroom. He went to check it out and a huge rat appeared. It ran away when he opened the door to the bathroom. Ton saw it climb up and disappear into the toilet and realized that it traveled from room to room through the sewer pipes. After this was reported to the band, we grew more cautious. We kept the toilet seats down at all times and flushed before using. Some of the band members even sealed their toilets with duct tape.

After one of our all night prayer times, Rick said he felt that we should go to the large Notre

Dame cathedral in the middle of the city and ask to talk to one of the priests. Rocky and I jumped in a rickshaw and headed for the Notre Dame Cathedral. The cathedral dominated a square in the center of the city and was the largest venue in Ho Chi Minh City.

We walked into the cathedral and I saw a young boy who looked like he was an altar boy. I asked him if I could see the priest. He took Rocky and I back behind the altar and pointed to a gravestone on the floor of the cathedral where a priest was buried. "No, I want to see the alive priest," I said. He looked at me like that was a strange request and walked away.

I looked around for another person to help me. I found someone else who looked like they belonged in the cathedral and asked to see the alive priest. He could comprehend the concept of seeing a living priest so he took us across the street to where the priest lived. He rang the doorbell and said something in Vietnamese. We were invited into a waiting room and were offered coffee before the priest entered the room.

As it turned out, the priest was actually the vice-vicar of Ho Chi Minh City. Father Nguyen oversaw many churches that had a total membership of over half a million people. His English was very good and he was obviously a well-educated, influential leader not only in the church, but also in Ho Chi Minh City.

"Father Nguyen, I want to thank you for taking the time to see us. We have been praying for three days and God told us to come and see you," I began. I explained our circumstances to him and that we were now here, but unable to do any concerts because the government refused to give us permission and would not release our equipment. "I believe that you are the man that will be able to help us," I concluded, hoping he would feel the same way.

He listened carefully and without hesitation said that he would help us. He offered to contact another priest and arranged for us to have a concert that evening. He asked me to see him again in a few days and told me he would set up several more concerts for us, including two concerts in Notre Dame Cathedral.

I asked Father Nguyen if he would pray for us and after he prayed, we thanked him and rushed back to the hotel to share the good news with the band. The only problem was we had only a matter of hours until our concerts and we had no equipment. No drums, no guitars, no amps, nothing.

It was at this moment that I recalled a television show called *The A-team*. It featured a group of experts and specialists who were sent out to quell the forces of crime. Often times this group appeared as a rag-tag bunch of incompetents, yet in their unorthodox ways surprised and caught the culprits with slick improvisational tactics. The A-Team was at their entertaining best using their ingenious creativity, innovation and versatility.

Even when it appeared their plans would fail, or when they were surprised by their enemies, they would change plans and do whatever it took to get the job done. They often looked disorganized, inefficient and bumbling, yet as the show concluded, every assignment was successfully completed, confounding the criminals and the law enforcement experts alike and making them heroes to the television audience. Always, at the end of each show, George Peppard, who played Hannibal Smith (the self-appointed leader of the A-Team), said, "I love it when a plan comes together."

"We've prayed and God has honored our prayers, now we must move quickly and do our jobs," I said. The band was fired up and ready for action.

Our hotel room was transformed into a war room as we made plans about how to be ready for a concert in just a few hours. It was 9 a.m. Saturday morning, so we had approximately six hours to find what we needed, negotiate prices, build the props and costumes, and transport everything to the church. No small task for foreigners in the chaos of Ho Chi Minh City. No sane person would have ever dreamed that we could get all that stuff in such a short period of time. But I was convinced that we would because I knew that God had miraculously opened this door for us.

By three o'clock in the afternoon, incredibly, the band had gathered all the equipment, props and costumes and were headed for the cathedral. All except for the coffin. Ho Chi Minh City is predominantly Buddhist and Buddhists are very superstitious about death. Ton Snelleart, who was responsible for special effects, had the precarious responsibility of buying a coffin and getting it to the cathedral. He found a coffin shop and inquired about buying one.

The first obstacle he faced was obvious as he had to answer the questions from the store owner,

Where is the body? Did you kill someone? Where are you taking the coffin? Ton found it extremely difficult to answer the questions since he spoke no Vietnamese and the owner spoke no English. A crowd started to congregate, curious about the strange request by this foreigner. One person was able to speak a little English and when all the questions were answered, finally a deal was made. Sixty dollars was the cost.

Ton then climbed in different coffins to determine the right size since the coffin needed to be at least six feet long and most Vietnamese were five feet. Procuring the right size, Ton tried to transport the coffin to the cathedral. Buddhists have a superstition about transporting coffins in their cars or vans. They believe it will bring them bad luck if they have a coffin in their vehicle. So no one was willing to transport the coffin. Ton, looked for a cyclo driver. These bicycle rickshaws are cheap and a common form of transportation throughout Ho Chi Minh City. The cyclo drivers are also very poor, so they gladly took the offer to taxi the coffin to the cathedral.

Shortly before the concert was to start and we were starting to worry about Ton and the coffin, we noticed a crowd moving like a wave down the busy street towards the cathedral. I saw the faces of horrified Vietnamese fleeing a cyclo with a coffin mounted on the front of it. It looked like the parting of the Red Sea. The people were afraid of the coffin, but also curious and after they ran away, they would return, fall in behind the cyclo and follow it to see where it was going. God used their curiosity as many from the crowd stayed for the concert.

After the concert, I preached to the crowd about Jesus and God's love for the Vietnamese people. Many people came to the front and prayed with us to begin a friendship with Jesus.

For the next two weeks God continued to give us opportunities to perform a total of ten times throughout the city. We were told that the secret police were always trying to figure out where we were going to go next so they could shut down our concerts, but we always managed to stay just ahead of them.

I was even invited by Father Nguyen to preach in the Notre Dame Cathedral. No foreigner had ever been allowed to speak before. I heard later that Mother Teresa had been unable to get permission to speak there.

Finally, we were preparing to do our biggest concert in the Notre Dame Cathedral before approximately 3,000 people. The church was completely packed, the aisles were full and people were hanging in the windows to see what was going on. After the concert's dramatic depiction of the crucifixion and resurrection, I invited those who wished to have a relationship with Jesus to come up on the altar. Because I didn't come from a Catholic background, I didn't realize that normally the priest is the only one allowed on the altar. I could tell that the people were afraid to come forward, so I looked at Father Nguyen and said, "Father Nguyen, is it OK for the people to come up on the altar." He said yes and a throng of people streamed forward and completely filled the large altar.

One day we were asked to go visit an orphanage and present a special program for the kids. Different members from the band juggled and did other things to entertain these kids. We brought them ice cream and balloons, and while I was explaining to them how they could know Jesus and just before I was going to invite them to pray with me, Jodi handed me a note that she had just been given. I opened it and it said, "You are not allowed to pray with these children." Apparently the secret police had caught up with us. I put the note in my pocket and said to the children, "I don't want anyone to pray now, but instead we are going to talk to God, but I don't want anyone to pray."

So the children and I talked to God together and many of them prayed for the first time. The secret police didn't stop us because apparently they were too stupid to figure out what we were doing.

On one of our last evenings there, we were invited to meet with the translators from the University. I was told that the English-speaking translators in the city all worked for the government as spies and I needed to be very careful about what we said or we could get ourselves in big trouble.

I told the band that we needed to be real low-key and not really talk about God, but just concentrate on being friends with them. We taught these students "The Yeah Song" in English and talked about America, but before long we were giving our testimonies and sharing about how Jesus had changed our lives. We ended up holding hands together in a circle and all the students prayed with us out loud and asked Jesus to come into their lives.

In spite of the fact that the government had canceled the friendship tour, we ended up doing more concerts and were able to tell thousands of people about God's love for them. God showed me once more that I need not look at the barriers or circumstances, but I need only to be willing to obey what God tells me to do.

CULT LEADER

IN GERMANY, OUR BRUCHSAL CONCERT WAS HELD at a maximum security prison where I had previously spoken. It's always a real joy to be in these high security prisons because it's so clear the God has a heart for the men there. While we were setting up for our concert, I was reminded of a high security prison we had played at in New Zealand. During a concert which was held in a gymnasium, different gang members stood and watched, acting both interested and disinterested at the same time. Just before we were about to begin another song, one of the prisoners handed me a piece of paper and asked if I would dedicate the next song to the Mongrel Mob, which is a violent gang in New Zealand. "This next song we're going to do is called, 'Love Instead' and it's dedicated to the Mongrel Mob," I declared. We began our song.

Members from the rival gang that was also attending our concert were not to be outdone so as soon as we finished 'Love Instead' I was handed another piece of paper by Black Power asking if I would dedicate the next song to them. "The next song we're going to play is called 'Jesus Says This' and it's dedicated to Black Power," I said.

When I held the microphone up to one of the gang members to get him to say "Hey" with me during the song, he pushed me away with his arm and the microphone almost went flying across the auditorium. It was at that point that I realized that I probably shouldn't encourage too much audience participation. So you never know what to expect when you play in a prison.

Half the inmates in Bruchsal are doing life sentences for murder. During the set up, I talked with the prison chaplain, Manfred, about my visit there a few months before. So many prisoners had responded when I had spoken that the prison newspaper wrote an article saying that I was a cult leader. So because of this negative press, there was much fear among the prisoners about coming to our concert. Still, about one-hundred prisoners came.

In the prison we had to do a shortened version of the "punk set," including the crucifixion scene.

They really laughed when we did the "No Sex" song, but it became more serious when we did the crucifixion scene. During the set, Jon Rush, our new bass player, slipped on the stage blood and fell on Hayden Kingdon, another band member, and cut open his chin, which then bled real blood. Ken Green, our drummer, also cut his leg when he slipped and fell on the drum kit. It was a very bloody concert!

When I gave an altar call, Claus came forward because he really wanted to make a stand in front of the other inmates. God had healed him of a nasty disease many years ago, and he had never forgotten this. While we prayed for strength for him the Holy Spirit broke him down, and he cried and recommitted his life to Christ.

Seeing the band had challenged Claus to make a stand for Christ in the prison, even though he was destined for a beating from the other prisoners. Manfred, had advised him that by standing up and coming forward, he would be hassled and be beaten a few times before the other prisoners forgot about it. But Claus really wanted to make a stand for God in the prison, despite the consequences.

Manfred called later to say that many prisoners wanted to come forward, but they were afraid.

At another concert in Kassel, Germany, there was a very heavy anti-Christ atmosphere that could be felt at the club where we had our concert. I've felt this often before in places like this. The walls contained posters of bands mocking God or promoting rebellion, destruction, and hopelessness.

Before the concert, I felt a lot of fear. I also felt sick to my stomach, which might have been caused by the fear. We were late in getting to the club. The sound man swore and screamed at us because we needed to change the stage that was already set up. We had to put our props where they needed to go. He was so angry he almost walked out, but I was able to get him to calm down and work with us.

The hardcore German band that played before we did was called Shattered Trust. Their music was quite heavy. The crowd looked heavy as well, especially a punk with a face covered in tattoos and pierced with many studs and rings. He was sitting on the stage drinking beer and seemed pretty drunk.

Once the concert started, the fear I had felt completely left me. One could literally feel the presence of God fall on the place. The hearts of the people really softened, and the heavy spirit that I felt beforehand just vanished. Even the sound man was softer and was touched by the concert.

The tattooed punk, Huga, was a lot more sober when we finished the concert. Jon talked to him, and Huga explained how the concert showed him the father-heart side of God. Jon asked Huga if he could pray with him, and he agreed. After Jon prayed, he gave Huga an NLM T-shirt and a Rock Priest book and put him in touch with a Christian center in Kassel.

Many other members of the band had similar conversations. It was a powerful night.

Broko, who was a leader in the squatter movement in Germany and a hard core anarchist, was having a birthday party on a farm in the German countryside. We were invited to perform our rock opera.

Unlike the Anarchy Festival I played at years earlier in Antwerp, Belgium, this was a very peaceful event. There was much hashish and alcohol being consumed, but everyone was very peaceful.

After our concert, Broko gave me a big hug and thanked us for coming. I was told that he was very anti-Christian, but I could tell that he was very touched by what he saw. I asked him if we could pray for him. So behind our tent, we gathered around Broko and asked that God would touch him.

THE JESUS CAMP

THE LORD BLESSED US WITH GOOD WEATHER IN WROCLAW, POLAND. Our concert was held at a square in the center of the city, and the sky looked as if it was going to rain all day. But as the concert started, the clouds moved away, and the blue sky shone through. The wind, which was also blowing quite hard, died down to next to nothing.

We were playing with Houk, a band led by Darek Malejonek, who prayed with me to receive Jesus after one of our first concerts in Poland in 1987. Houk was now a popular band on the Polygram record label. Darek speaks openly about Jesus now from the stage. He had just given his testimony before 100,000 people at a big gathering earlier that summer.

After the concert, I talked about the need to be saved and how God loves Poland. About one-thousand people listened quietly. One-hundred and twenty people came to the stage to receive Christ. I had them hold hands and form a big circle while I led them in a prayer of salvation. Before leaving, different members of the band gave them flyers inviting them to the Jesus Camp.

This scene was repeated after every concert we did in Poland.

Peter was a typical 20-year-old atheist who attended our concert at the Stodola club in Warsaw, Poland. He told Hayden Kingdon, a Steiger missionary to Europe, that he found the concert interesting but he didn't believe in any kind of God. Hayden felt that Peter was curious about us, so he invited him to come to the Jesus Camp. Peter, along with three-hundred and ten others, registered for the Jesus Camp in Gyzicko, Poland.

The Jesus Camp was for those who wanted to know more about God after seeing our concerts. Most of those attending were in their early twenties with little or no church background. During the Jesus Camp, we had workshops and seminars as well as evangelistic concerts in the evening for the general public.

After I gave a talk about God's forgiveness, Peter came forward for prayer. He wasn't ready to ask Jesus into his life, but he wanted to talk.

The next night during the evangelistic concert, we asked those who were interested to come forward to the stage to accept Jesus into their hearts. Peter went forward that night with many others and asked Jesus to come into his life!

About three-hundred people like Peter gave their lives to Jesus or made new steps toward God. The last night, we asked those who had made a decision to follow Jesus to come to the stage and light a candle. Several hundred Polish young people stood in the cool evening air holding candles, worshipping God. It was an awesome sight!

Jodi talking after a concert

RETURN TO YUGOSLAVIA

WHILE THE REST OF THE BAND WAS INVOLVED WITH FOL-
LOW UP IN GERMANY, Jodi and I traveled to Serbia
(Yugoslavia) to begin preparations for a concert tour
there for Elephant, another ministry band that was
working with us and to meet Davor, a refugee we
had been corresponding with for almost a year. It
had been nearly twenty years since I had last been
to Yugoslavia and I was really looking forward to
the trip, but at the same time, I felt a certain amount
of apprehension. We had just heard reports on the
news that Belgrade was on the verge of collapse
and daily there were new reports about outbreaks
of violence and general anarchy throughout the
country.

I also had a very strange experience when I applied to get a visa for Serbia in Germany, which added to my insecurity.

It was the typical scene in the Yugoslavian consulate. It was crowded with people applying for visas and Jodi, Laura, the drummer for Elephant, and I were waiting our turn when suddenly a Serbian man somewhere in his early fifties marched out of the office straight towards me. His eyes were ablaze with anger and he pointed to me, crossed himself, and told me to get out. I was stunned and I raised my hands in protest of his irrational behavior. It seemed that if I protested too much, he would physically strike me. I started to walk towards the door, feeling like he was about to push me out onto the sidewalk, but instead he slammed the door behind me and locked it.

To say the least, I was somewhat stunned and concerned because they had my passport, but fortunately, Jodi and Laura were still there and they still presented them with all three of our passports and visas to get into the country.

When Jodi and I arrived in Belgrade, I was a little nervous but was soon relieved to find the city peaceful, at least on the surface. While we were waiting for our train to Novi Sad, where Davor lived, we struck up a conversation with a young man in his early twenties from Croatia. He was very excited about our band and was very interested in organizing a tour in Croatia.

When we arrived in Novi Sad, it was getting close to dark and I was anxious to get settled in a hotel as I had heard it wasn't too safe to be out on the streets at night. We found a hotel next to the train station, where they gladly gave us a room and charged us double the normal price because we were from the West. We had been given the name of a pastor in the city, Alexander, who I called and who agreed to meet us the next day.

"Don't discuss Serbia or the Orthodox Church or you could get yourself shot!" Alexander warned us, as we walked the streets of Novi Sad. This was a city full of refugees from the war in Bosnia. Alexander had received death threats against his children because he was a pastor of a local church in the city.

A young student from Alexander's church helped us to locate Davor. I felt that God wanted us to find him. We followed a dusty path to a filthy bungalow and knocked on the door. Davor's mother met us at the door. She was bent over from years of hard labor.

"Is Davor there?" I asked. She looked at us suspiciously and called Davor.

"Is that you, David?" he gasped, not really believing it and slightly at a loss for words. After the shock wore off, we decided to go for a walk. "You better pick up some stones in case we run into rabid dogs," he explained. So, Jodi and I looked for two good-sized stones, just in case.

He began to describe how they were lucky to have escaped Mostar, Bosnia when they did. Many of his friends had been killed, and he and his brother and mother were lucky to be in Novi Sad alive. Jodi and I were moved as he described the struggles he had endured but mostly by his passion for God. "I've asked God if I can share Jesus with a million people in my lifetime!" he said.

Later, we were invited for dinner by his mother. We were surprised to find only two plates at the dinner table, although five of us were supposed to be eating. We discovered that this was common practice when they invited guests to their home for dinner in Novi Sad. The guests would eat, and whatever was left over was what everyone else would get to eat.

During our trip there, we were able to get the invitations for Elephant to go back a few weeks later, and we made preparations for working with Davor in the future.

After our concert tour in Europe, we traveled to Singapore where we did two concerts in a large theater where an Anglican church meets. Because it's illegal to tell Moslems about Jesus there, we invited those who were interested in knowing more about Him after our concerts to sign up to be a part of the No Longer Music fan club. Four hundred young people signed up. And Steiger has a permanent ministry presence in the Singapore hardcore music scene today.

Despite illness, corrupt officials, and just about everything else that could try to stop us, our world tour ended in Goa, India. At Christmas, the band organized a big breakfast in a nearby slum. Each day we held evangelistic concerts, sometimes in strange venues like a law school or a posh tourist resort. We also had open Bible studies on the beach and visited bars and other clubs so that we could get to know people and begin to build relationships.

Everywhere we went we saw God do mighty things and open up even more opportunities for ministry in the future. I'm beginning to understand more and more that you can go anywhere with Jesus.

SOLDIER OR CIVILIAN?

"WHY, WHEN THERE IS SUCH A GREAT POTENTIAL HARVEST, are there so few workers?"

I posed this question to the student body at Northwestern College in St. Paul, Minnesota, in 1992. It was a question that had been on my mind for several years.

Standing on the platform in the main auditorium, I continued: "Jesus said in Matthew 9:37 that 'the harvest is plentiful, but the workers are few.' Why? How can this be? Why are there so few workers?"

I told the students that as I had traveled around the world I had seen that there was an enormous spiritual hunger and that God has a broken heart

for you, God. I love to play music. I want to play music for you.'

"But a soldier says, 'Tell me what to do with my life. I don't care what it is. Whatever you want me to do, I will do it.' There is a tremendous difference."

I told the students that I always enjoyed my trips back to Minnesota, and I particularly relished taking long walks in the local woods.

"One day as I was walking," I continued, "I was praying to God. 'God you know I'd love to have a house. I've been living in the inner city of Amsterdam for thirteen years now. If my little boys want to ride their bicycles, I have to take them in a car to the outskirts of the city. I have to tell them, when they are on the streets, not to touch the needles lying there in the gutter so they won't get AIDS. I never grew up in a place like this. I was raised where everyone had their own house with plenty of space.'

"As I expressed my heart to God I felt he was pleased with my prayer. I felt as though God said that he too would love for me to have a house, (and maybe some day I will)[1]. But as I was walking, something rose up within me and I said, 'But God,

---

[1] In 1997, David and Jodi Pierce were able to finally build a house for their family — on the beach in New Zealand.

if you want me to live in that tiny apartment in Amsterdam for the rest of my life, I'm willing to do that because I want to be a soldier.'

"A soldier is under orders. He's not self-directed. And he trusts the commanding officer with his life.

"Have you believed the great lie that God wants us always to be feeling good, rich and prosperous? Is that how we know we are in God's will? When things are going well, is it a sign that God is happy with us? That's not what Jesus said.

"In John 16:33, Jesus said, 'In this world you will have trouble, but take heart. I have overcome the world.'

"I can remember coming back to the hotel on one of our tours in Moscow," I said. "I felt like I needed to get away by myself and cry for a whole day. Why did I feel this way? Was it because the tour was difficult? Yes, in many ways, the tour had been difficult. But that wasn't the reason I wanted to cry.

"Was it because I missed my family? Yes, I really missed my family. But that wasn't the reason I wanted to cry.

"Was it because I was exhausted? Yes, I was exhausted, but that wasn't the reason I wanted to cry.

"The reason I wanted to cry was that I was over-whelmed with the privilege that God had given me to go into the harvest field. I thought, *God, why are you allowing me to do this? You see who I am. You see my struggles and imperfections? Why are you giving me the privilege of seeing the kinds of things that I am seeing?*

"The greatest thing we can do with our lives is to go into the harvest fields. There is no greater privilege than to be a part of God's army. I believe, as a Christian, that there is a broad road and a nar-row way, just as Jesus taught. There is a 'broad road that leads to destruction and many people find it.' But he also said, 'there is a narrow way that leads to life.'

"In the Christian life too, there is a broad road and a narrow way. We can live good lives, be in-volved in a church and God will love us. God doesn't love me *more* if I work with starving people in Calcutta than if I'm an insurance salesman in Minneapolis.

"God doesn't love us for what we do for him. I love my two little boys because they are my two little boys and for no other reason. But God is look-ing for people who are willing to take a small part of his broken heart for the world. He is looking for people who are willing to take the narrow way that he offers them.

"God is not looking for super Christians, but for those who believe that Jesus is worthy of our best. Some of you are going to wake up one morning in old age, sitting in your home and saying, 'If only I had taken the narrow way that God offered me. If only I hadn't settled for second best.'

"I believe there are many civilians whom God is calling to be soldiers. If this word is for you, I invite you to come forward and kneel with me here on the stage."

Several hundred students came to the stage, and others filled the aisles as they volunteered to be a part of God's army.

CAN I ASK YOU THE SAME QUESTION I ASKED THOSE STUDENTS? Are you a soldier or a civilian? The way you answer can change not only your life, but also history!

epilogue

AK-47
by Jake Chaya

SMEARED ACROSS A WALL IN A DARK NIGHTCLUB CALLED AK-47, in Dusseldorf, Germany, were foot-high words, "666...he is the real. Jesus was only a fool on a hill." Disgusted, I turned to another wall to see scrawled in red, "Jesus Christ died for his own sins, not mine." Rage churned in my stomach.

My eyes shot from wall to wall. I saw a picture of two ugly demons tearing apart a baby. On the stage, a pile of skeletons with "Lost Babylon" branded on one skull burst from the wall.

"Looks like a great place to meet Satan," I mumbled. No Longer Music huddled silently and stared at the walls.

We were finishing a six-concert tour in Germany in November 1992. Violent confrontation between radical right-wing gangs and their prey had occurred across Germany. They had been violently protesting Germany's acceptance of refugees, and foreigners had been their targets. Compounding our trouble, liberal anti-Christian crowds had mocked the band and cursed and jeered at the Christian lyrics.

David was no stranger to this culture. He and his band had toured Siberia, Mongolia, Russia and Islamic Republics in the Soviet Union for two years and had grown accustomed to the non-Christian culture. But as we unloaded the band equipment, I knew David was concerned.

AK-47 was in a dangerous location. Squatters had taken over a few blocks of an old building and had been so resistant that Dusseldorf city officials had legally surrendered the buildings to them. "Them" meant drug dealers and addicts. This street had a notorious reputation. Within minutes, I concurred: the reputation was true.

We had passed a statue of welded pipe, twisted metal, American soldier's helmets, chains and wire at the building's entrance. Inside, obscenely graffitied walls were covered by posters of bands with names like Sharon Tate's Children, Lethal Gospel, The Bone Club, Bimbo Krauts, Unsane Surgeons, The Two Party Dictators and Multiple

Personality Disorders. I alternately prayed and asked myself why I had come.

For years, David and No Longer Music had gone where the Gospel has not yet been heard and accepted. But at AK-47, I felt God had been rejected. "Stay out!" the place screamed. "We've heard about Jesus Christ and we don't believe in Him, nor do we accept those who do!" For the first time in my life, I feared to speak of my beliefs. The listeners wouldn't merely ignore me — verbal or physical attack was possible. My pride in being an American and Christian vanished. I was now an object of scorn. There were no safe places to run.

The crew finished setting up the equipment and completed the sound check. I squinted into the dark, unheated room in disbelief. "How could people stray so far away from God?" I asked myself. "What's made them so angry and hateful toward Jesus Christ?" I looked at the ceiling and saw another message, "No Masters, No God." What would it be like in two hours when NLM loudly proclaimed that God loves His people so much that He sent His son Jesus to die for them?

The crew had been too busy to worry, but two of the women from the band look afraid and restless. One shot me a forced smile. I could see in her eyes that she was counting on the crew to protect her. Could we? I had little faith in myself and the band. I hoped God would protect us, but fear predominated.

A group of nine Christians living in Dusseldorf had provided us with food and helped us set up our equipment. Andreas had been their leader for eight years, yet only one person in the neighborhood had committed her life to following Jesus Christ. Andreas, a peaceful fellow who reminded me of the apostle John, knew the street culture intimately. I asked how the people responded to his work and how they reacted when he told them about Jesus. "People took a long time to warm up to Jesus." Andreas said. "But the team feels a breakthrough is near. Perhaps this concert will be the catalyst."

We had prayed with Andreas' team in the coffee house an hour ago. As I listened to the different prayers, I sensed a new boldness in David and the band, yet humbleness toward God. It didn't matter how scared we were, we were in God's hands now. David prayed, "I don't care what these people say, I don't care what they do, what matters is what God says, and God says for us to love Him, then to love one another."

That had sounded easy when I'd heard those words in a suburban Minneapolis church. But was I ready to confront hostility with what I believed, and love these people, too?

I was glad I was working the video equipment and not performing. Perhaps I wouldn't be noticed. I knew God was teaching me a lesson in faith and commitment as I walked through the smoke-filled crowded audience to my position.

People stared at my No Longer Music t-shirt. One tall woman with matted red and purple hair and heavy makeup smiled as I tested the video player. I smiled weakly. What could she be thinking? I inserted my earplugs, set the first tape and glanced to my left. The floor was sticky with beer, and in the dim light I saw people inhaling cigarettes, hash pipes and joints. I tried to look busy.

Suddenly an explosion of sound filled the darkened club. I switched the video to "Freedom" and turned to watch David approach the stage. Wearing a hard-hat with three brilliant white lights shining out at different angles, he jumped onto the smoke-filled stage. I looked at the crowd. Eyes darted about as people tried to capture the big-screened lyrics, lights, smoke, the video projection, David and the band members. Sight and sound were like thunder and lightning. The crowd responded with dancing and gestures toward the stage. Music and special effects bathed the walls.

On this tour, No Longer Music was using a 12-song set, followed by a dramatization of the Gospel. David would conclude by speaking to the audience about what the drama meant and what Jesus Christ can do for each one of us, if we accept Christ as our personal Savior. Enhancing the music and drama were special effects: strobe light, smoke and high-powered stage lights synchronized with the message of each song. A large screen projected the lyrics in German so audiences could understand exactly what David sang about.

As the set progressed, people looked more to the screen with the lyrics. The audience seemed to divide. One group, young Christians, part of Andreas' team and their friends read the German lyrics, attentive and enthusiastic. In the other group, two skinheads, a large number of headbangers and about eight burly slam dancers mocked the lyrics, pushed and shoved. I was hit by bodies four times and twice the video equipment was jolted.

"God, don't let anything break, including me!" In answer to my prayer, three of Andreas' team formed a wall between the dancers and me so the equipment could be protected.

The set concluded and the drama began. David and his band acted out God's creation of the world, how Satan rebelled and was cast out of God's kingdom and how Satan set out to ruin mankind. The drama progressed to show God sending His son Jesus to earth and how Satan used the evil in people to kill Jesus.

The Christians in the audience had been silent during the drama. Others in the crowd had grown angry. From different areas of the audience, mocking laughter, cursing and angry shouts of sarcasm penetrated the club. The crowd noise level built. David used modern symbols in the drama, so the crucifixion scene showed him being fastened to a microphone stand cross and electrocuted by large battery cables. The audience was riveted. As David portrayed Jesus dead on the cross, the unbelievers in the crowd cheered his death. One yelled, "hallelujah" and obscenities rang out.

"You jerks!" I yelled back. "Oh, God," I instantly prayed "what if they come after me?" The headbangers ignored me and claimed victory as David was laid in the coffin. Moments later, David broke through the coffin as the risen Christ. The

Christians cheered. Others whistled and booed, some cursed, others turned away in disgust, shaking their heads vehemently.

Then David grabbed a microphone. I saw a strength and courage I've never witnessed in anyone. Despite the taunts, cursing, and angry outbursts, David reiterated what had taken place in the drama. David then spoke about how each person in the hall needed to fill the emptiness in his heart. He illustrated how pride often causes people, including himself before he'd known Jesus, to look to drugs, sex, alcohol, worship fake gods and expect others to fill the emptiness. He boldly stated that nothing but a relationship with Jesus Christ could fill that emptiness. He asked Andreas and his team to come to the stage. David invited the audience members to come and talk to the band or Andreas' team if they wanted to know more about Jesus.

We waited for a response. No one came to the stage. David asked again. Someone yelled a comment in German, others laughed, but David still gazed into the crowd.

No one had come forward, but the Christians in the audience had moved back to talk to the people who had yelled and laughed at David. David thanked everyone and walked off the stage.

I felt defeated.

Suddenly the crowd erupted. They wanted NLM to play an encore. David told me to put in a new videotape. NLM played again. No one left.

I no longer felt defeated, afraid or angry. As the crowd responded and I watched the band talk with the crowd, I knew that God was at work.

After the crowd left, as we packed the equipment, David and I had a moment to reflect on the night's events. "I was really impressed with your love of God. You really don't care what anyone thinks or says, do you?" I commented. "And weren't Andreas and his team great?"

David agreed, "Andreas' team are warriors!"

David continued. "Christians get too comfortable speaking only to people who are willing to listen. They need to talk to people who need Jesus, but don't know it yet."

"I prayed for people to listen during the drama. How did you feel when people shouted and mocked you?"

David laughed, "It doesn't bother me. In today's world so many people have turned so far away from God that they don't know who or what to believe in. That's why they come to places like AK-47. People will talk easily about believing in crystals, trees, animals, statues and people, but then when you talk about Jesus Christ, they get angry. This has always been the case throughout Christian history."

I nodded in agreement, then David went on. "When I come to an AK-47, I expect people to get angry, curse, shout and mock me. Hey, sometimes they spit in my face. But God knows that I love Him so much that I'll let them spit on me if that's what it takes to get people to hear about Jesus Christ."

With tears in my eyes, I said, "Amen."

Club AK-47

A Steiger International Board Member, Jake Chaya accompanied David Pierce and the band No Longer Music on their six-concert tour of Germany in 1992.

24

BAND VAMPIRE
by David Pierce

Jodi came on stage dressed in a long red dress wrapped up in a black veil. She had a doll tucked into the veil in order to make her look pregnant. She slowly walked up to the guitar players in a mummy-like trance. Our two guitar players took the two ends of the veil and slowly unwrapped her to reveal the doll. She placed the doll in a noose which was hanging on stage.

After getting rid of the doll, she picked up the veil and begin to wrap and twist her daughter in it against her will. Finished for the moment with tormenting her daughter, she went to her husband and led him into putting his neck through the noose in order to kill him too.

Having accomplished that, she considered it a very good day and was content to finish off the day decorating the place where her husband was hanging and ending her time with her daughter by pretending to give her a birthday cake but instead smashing it as she placed it before her and laughed hysterically. As the scene ended, Jodi returns to sit with her dead husband enjoying her moment of triumph.

For Ton Snelleart who was playing her dead husband, this wasn't that strange since he was officially the band vampire. Having a band vampire was one of the things that made me feel very good about our 1996 World Tour. Not that Ton really was a vampire, it was just that he looked like a vampire. He wasn't trying to look like a vampire, God just made him that way. And as you know having someone in your band who looks like a vampire is a very cool thing.

Ton, who was from Amsterdam, joined up with me when he started coming to the church we started in our boat behind central station in Amsterdam. I invited him to do special effects for No Longer Music, which he agreed to do and came with us when we relocated to Wellington, New Zealand. He was involved in the drug scene and the gay community for many years before he gave his life to Jesus. He used to dress up like a space man or pirate and walk the streets of Amsterdam.

He had a friend named Wolf who operated a pirate radio station called Radio Death. Wolf recorded all the people who called him up to complain about the station. "This is terrible, how can you put such sick things on the radio?" one woman would complain. "Your radio program is the most disgusting thing I have ever heard!" remarked another irate caller. He would play these calls at the beginning of his radio program with background noises of machine guns killing people that complained. One of the popular topics on his programs was different ways to make fun of Jesus and blaspheme God.

About the same time, Ton had opened an art gallery where he was painting cosmic consciousness art and selling drugs. There was a new age woman who came to visit him. She had two dice. On one side it said "Jesus Christ Yes" and on the other side it said "Jesus Christ No." As she was walking down the street and she was trying to decide whether to cross the street, she would roll the dice. If the dice said "Jesus Christ Yes" she would cross the street and if the dice said "Jesus Christ No" she wouldn't. She would often visit Ton's art gallery and tell Ton about the Transit. Jesus was going to come back on a white horse together with his rainbow warriors to the middle of the Atlantic Ocean and only certain people would be transported.

Ton wanted to know if he could find the kingdom of God so she rolled the dice ten times and each time it said "Jesus Christ No." This freaked Ton out and made him frightened and desperate.

In the meantime, Wolf was sitting in his room and as he described it, an angel came through the wall and rebuked him for his radio show and the way he was making fun of Jesus. Wolf came to Ton and told him what happened, saying only Ton would believe it.

This of course made Ton even more desperate. One day someone came to his art gallery to buy some cocaine. He said, "I would like to buy a gram of cocaine, but I don't have any money."

Ton asked, "Well what do you have to trade for it?"

The guy offered Ton a New Testament. Because of the recent events that had been occurring in Ton's life, he eagerly accepted the deal and traded a gram of cocaine for the New Testament. Ton and his friend from the radio station started the gutter church which had only two members — themselves. For one year they read the Bible together in his "cave" near Vondelpark.

During this time, God completely transformed Ton's life, forgave him for all the bad things he was involved in, set him free from his drug addiction and his homosexuality. Now he is a full time member of No Longer Music. When he is not on tour with the band, he runs a home for destitute people in Delhi, India that we started in 1997.

TON PLAYING THE DEAD HUSBAND IN THE ABOVE SCENE WAS PART OF *PASSION (AN ACT OF)*. Our band performed this on our world tour which included twenty five concerts in seven countries over three months. This rock opera tells of a young couple getting tempted into adultery, sandwiched in between are lots of juicy bits, like suicide, physical abuse, guns, tarty blondes, despair and a Satan figure gleefully singing shock lyrics like "Rape, rape, rape, celebrate your rape by your father."

During this chaos and despair Jesus comes onto the scene to show that he has answers for all this brokeness. During the show I play Jesus and I'm tortured and then shot in the head, execution style, by the unfaithful husband.

Soon afterwards a seven foot tall death angel played by Damaris Kingdon dances on the stage celebrating the death of Jesus. But her joy turns to horror as the resurrected Jesus emerges from the smoky pandemonium.

That night we were in Auckland, New Zealand, towards the beginning of our World Tour. I felt a real broken heart for the lost kids who were in the audience. As I explained the message of the cross after the performance, there was a rush to the front of the stage of people making a commitment to Christ or young Christians rededicating their lives to God.

One of those who gave his life to Jesus that evening had earlier asked for a refund before our concert started. The organizer convinced him to watch the first ten minutes of our show. If he didn't like it, then they would refund the ticket. After watching the first ten minutes, he changed his mind and decided to stay. He was the last one to come forward after the concert to receive Jesus as his personal Savior.

Ton Snelleart

25

FIRST AVENUES

by Stephen Knight

I'M NOT ONE OF THOSE PEOPLE WHO DOESN'T "DO" STARBUCK'S BECAUSE THEY'RE TOO "CORPORATE." However I must admit, I'm still rather particular when it comes to the coffee joints I frequent. Jitters is too trendy. Kuppernicus is too artsy. The Purple Onion is too grungy. But Starbuck's in Edina[2]? Now that's a little out of my league. As in, I would never choose to go hang out here in a strip mall, at a coffeehouse franchise like Starbuck's (the McDonald's of coffeehouses, as a friend put it).

But it's not my choice. I'm having coffee with David Pierce. You know, the "Rock Priest"? You

---

[2] A wealthy suburb of Minneapolis.

might know him from books such as *They Call Him...Rock Priest*. Well anyways, he's got that long, frizzy Joey Ramone hair with bangs[3] (sans the dark sunglasses, at least on this occasion). He'd actually fit in pretty well in a police line-up with Joey, Steve Taylor and Mike Roe of the 77's. At least I wouldn't know which one looked more like a criminal.

Well, David Pierce is, in all actuality, an old punk rocker. Yeah, like Joey Ramone. Except Joey is still doing the same old thing, and David Pierce? Well, he's got a new thing going, and he's going to tell me all about it. But first I'm thinking David looks exactly like he did when I first met him in '92.

I was involved with the "Hardcore Bible Study," meeting in a vacant funeral home, inviting all the suburban punks to study the word of God. It was an interesting time. By the time I met David, the Bible study had moved into a church basement, and the leaders were considering turning it into an outreach of Steiger International - the organization David started years before on "the boat" (Steiger 14) back in Amsterdam.

---

[3] They call it "Fringe" in New Zealand.

I had read all about it in the pioneer, underground Christian zines like *White Throne* and *The Cutting Edge*. Later I got the whole story in the *Rock Priest* book. Pretty legendary stuff.

Well David Pierce was there, in the flesh, speaking one night in the basement, and we all went out to Ember's afterwards - because everyone was sick of Perkin's by this time. Anyways, the service was horrible, but the food was good. I guess the management was freaked out about a bunch of young "punks" (we were hardly that scary-looking) coming in and commandeering a big table. Oh well. So I interviewed David about his band, No Longer Music, and what they're all about. I published the interview in the first "serious" issue of my magazine, *Kamikaze*. I say "serious" because it was at this point that I had decided to turn *Kamikaze* into a full-on arts and entertainment magazine "from a Christian perspective," of course.

I had kept in touch over the last few years, sending copies of *Kamikaze* overseas to Mr. Pierce for his reading enjoyment. Then one day, I received a long e-mail message from him, via his personal assistant Kaye Kirsch, concerning a certain review of the movie *Pulp Fiction* which I had printed,

Dear Stephen,

During my recent travels I saw a movement of phony radical Christians. Ones that think they are being radical not because of the stand they take, but because of the stand they don't take. Not because of showing the Jesus standard and being willing to live the consequences of it, but instead they think they are radical because they see how close to the world's standard they can be and still call themselves Christians.

These phony alternative Christians present a watered-down gutless Jesus that attracts compromising Christians at the same time presenting a toothless Christianity to the world that no one respects. The decision Kamikaze *has to make is: Are you going to align yourselves with true radical Christianity which takes a stand and lifts up a higher standard? Or are you going to join the multitudes of phony radicals?*

When I read the review on Pulp Fiction *it appears that you are choosing to join the ranks of the phony radicals. In the article, it states,* "Pulp Fiction *has achieved unprecedented criti-*

cal and commercial success. As a result standards and moral guidelines often become gray whenever anyone analyzes secular art forms from a Christian perspective." When do Christian standards and moral guidelines ever become gray? Jesus was never confused about standards. He ate with sinners, and we need to do the same. But He still told them the truth. He identified with their questions, their longings, their pain and suffering but he did not identify with their sin...

Steve, forgive me for the harshness of this letter. I just don't want you to join the ranks of watered down Christian movements that I have seen. Don't be afraid to have standards. In the letterhead of your magazine, you say, "Kamikaze Magazine, Arts and literature from a different perspective." Do it! Don't be afraid to give the Jesus perspective and don't think that you're not being open or that you're judgmental if you don't give lip service to the world's perspective.

He said he was going to be in Minneapolis for one of his speaking engagements, and he wanted to get together. So here they were, David and Kaye, by the back wall of the commercial coffee bistro in up scale Yuppie-land. He was looking like Joey Ramone again. Little did I know that two months from then I would be married and I'd be buying my new sister-in-law a Starbuck's To-Go mug.

I came in, prepared to bite the bullet. What David had said hit home for me. Though I was prepared to defend my decision to print the review of *Pulp Fiction*, and ultimately defend everything I was doing with *Kamikaze*, in a strange way I was also ready to throw in the towel and tell old David Pierce, "You got me! That's right, you got me. Enough's enough, already. I'm done with the magazine business." I had just gotten sick of all the rigmarole — the writing, the selling, the distribution, the schmoozing. It was all so life-consuming. And for what?

A few new people came to church because they heard about it in *Kamikaze*. A few people got involved with a Bible study because the heard about it in *Kamikaze*. Nobody was inspired to become a missionary by reading *Kamikaze*. Nobody go saved by reading *Kamikaze* - at least, none that I know of. In short, *Kamikaze* accomplished none of the things that I had always been taught were really important

- evangelism and discipleship. People just read the darn thing, and then they recycled. I was beginning to feel like it wasn't much of a "ministry" at all. I was pretty discouraged. It was time for me to reduce.

But I still had a passion in me to shake things up - in a good way. I wholeheartedly agreed with Pierce when he said in the first interview, "It's good that there are Christian bands for Christians to listen to, but there needs to be more evangelistic bands. 99.9% of Christian music is entertainment."

Now, I didn't exactly know what evangelism was, at least not in the hands-on sense of the term. I would probably consider myself an evangelical Christian, and for years I did *Kamikaze* and called it a "pre-evangelistic" tool to spreading the Gospel among the dread Generation X. But what was I talking about? I had never led anyone to the Lord in my life. No jewels in my crown, at least not yet.

So when David Pierce gets to talking about evangelism and the state of Christian music, I get excited because I know he's on-to-it. He's in synch with the Spirit. He may be 40-something, but he's not out-of-touch. So he tells me about the World Tour NLM is embarking on the next summer, and then he says two startling things, like two earth-shattering, mind-blowing things.

"We need a journalist to come with us and write a book about the tour," he says. "Will you go?"

At this time I was shocked. This was a big decision. One of those you have to "sleep on" — and talk to your fiancé about, of course. But I was reminded of his own words form that interview years before: "The most important thing you will do for God is the next thing He asks you to do."

Why? "Because when I say no to God about that next thing, no matter how insignificant that step looks to me, it slows down my (spiritual) growth. The more I'm willing to yield to God and take that next step, the faster I'm going to grow."

I was challenged. I was convicted. And I knew I was ready for that next step. If this was what God was asking me to do, I would do it.

"We want to play in Minneapolis," David continued. "We want to play at First Avenue."

Now, I might have had some influence in the Christian music scene, but First Avenue was something else. To me, First Avenue was a big, scary scene — the biggest live music venue in the Twin Cities. And it was everything that the Christian scene wasn't — tattooed, pierced and proud. In short, it was a fortress of darkness too heavy for me (or any Christian artist for that matter) to penetrate. And the Mainroom, no less. I mean, only the "big" bands play there. This is where I saw Moby rave on, the Afghan Whigs rock on, and G. Love roll on. I may have had a few Christian friends in the club (moving covertly in the scene), but I was afraid my connections weren't strong enough to pull a band as unknown and unpopular as No Longer Music into the Mainroom.

"I mean, let's face it," I thought to myself, "most people don't even know who No Longer Music is, and those who have heard of them, think they're a cheesy Christian rock band. Sure, they do some wacky stuff on stage, performing in front of mostly 'secular,' sometimes even hostile audiences, reaping the harvest of many young lives for Christ — but that'll never go over at First Avenue."

Or would it? I was about to find out.

WITH ONLY A FEW WEEKS BEFORE NLM WOULD ARRIVE IN THE STATES from New Zealand, I found myself frantically trying to set up a concert for them in a park or a club or somewhere. Anywhere.

It was a slow afternoon in the *Bulletin* newspaper office where I worked answering the phones (i.e.

"editorial assistant"). It might have been the first time in my life I truly cried out to God for His clear guidance and direction.

The concert in Minneapolis was a key part of the tour, and it was entirely my responsibility. If I have ever in my life heard the "still small voice" of God, it was then.

"Go to First Avenue. If I want NLM to play there, I'm God, and I'll take care of it."

It was that simple, and yet profound.

When I got home from work that day, there was a message on my voice-mail from Nathan, a child-hood friend and a core member of Steiger Minneapolis' ministry team. We went to Christian school together, and he was there when I got baptized in the coffin down at Lake Calhoun —it was the strange sort of shocking, symbolic thing that Steiger people did.

"Steve, call me. I think there's a way we can get NLM in at First Avenue."

AROUND 1 A.M., BECKY AND I WERE LOADING THE NLM TEAM into a van fresh from their flight - New Zealand to L.A., L.A. to Denver, and (five hours later) Denver to Minneapolis. We knew that over the next week or so we would be trying frantically to pack up our young married lives and keep the team busy while in Minneapolis.

For some, this was their first time in the U.S. and in Minneapolis of all places. That meant one thing: the Mall of America. On more that one occasion.

It must have been an interesting sight, Becky and I trying to keep the motley International Team from flying apart at the seams. The flamboyant Ton Snellaert, artistic director for the rock opera, was the consummate anti-consumer, but he did score a new pair of crazy sunglasses to go with his ensemble of clownish attire. Other team members bought surfing gear - for the "incredible waves" off the shores of India, later on in the tour. NLM's drummer, Ken Green, picked up what would become a prize possession (and a steadfast source of amusement during the tour) - a talking watch.

We would forever remember the familiar sound of the watch. *"Cock-a doodle-do! The time is 10:09 pm."*

ON FRIDAY NIGHT, WE WERE INVITED OUT TO SCANDIA, MINNESOTA, for a real American barbecue at Art and Emily Montgomery's house. The Montgomery's were old friend of David's dating back to his days at "Everybody's House," a Bible study he led at the University of Minnesota in the late '70s until it ended in controversy.

The 15-passenger van we were borrowing from Nathan's church had broken down twice that day, and our tensions for the concert at First Avenue, now just two days away, were running high.

At the time, it seemed like freak circumstances, but later I discovered that NLM is cursed by bad transportation in just about every country they visit. Looking back now, I have fond memories of those times, parked on the shoulder of Highway 35W, backed up with rush hour traffic, people heading north for the weekend.

When we finally arrived at the Montgomery's (by car, not van), our friends from Steiger Minneapolis were already there waiting for us. We gathered around a bonfire in the yard, and Hayden Kingdon sang some of the worship songs he had written for Steiger New Zealand.

"Holy Spirit, come inside/ by Your power change my life/ and ease my struggling inside."

My heart truly felt the Holy Spirit's crushing calm. I was "humbled but not betrayed." God gave me a peace about the nagging transportation situation and a promise that it would be resolved.

The night was not only important for me, but also for strengthening the bond between Steiger International and the rag-tag Steiger Minneapolis team. Many of the people from the "Geek Squad" (as David affectionately referred to Steiger Minneapolis) were preparing to leave the next day for the "Rainbow Gathering" - a hippie festival attended by thousands held in a national forest every year.

Steiger Minneapolis director Mark Johnson had first heard about the Gathering through people at the Hard Times Cafe on the West Bank in Minneapolis. In 1995, a team for Steiger Minneapolis went to the Gathering for the first time, setting up a "Jesus Kitchen" where hippies and punks were fed and where they held worship each night. They had been planning for a whole year to go again.

David had urged them to support the concert on Sunday, even if that meant going a day later to the Gathering. I know Nathan and others were torn by the conflict, but they felt certain they should go to the Gathering. This night was an important time of prayer and worship for us all. We prayed for our brothers and sisters in the "Geek Squad," and Art Montgomery shared from his heart.

It was like a heavy sword in my hands.

"I'm reminded of the movie *Glory*," he began, "which tells the story of an all-black army regiment that was very successful during the Civil War. So when the North was going to attack a Confederate stronghold that was nearly impenetrable, and there was only a narrow way to attack, this brigade was the only one to volunteer to lead the charge. The night before they went into battle, they sat around a fire in their camp, just like we are, and sang and worshipped together, knowing that tomorrow they would most surely die..."

WHEN SUNDAY ROLLED AROUND, I didn't know what to expect. We had tried to book local bar bands to open for NLM, but the club ruled them out. It seemed ironic at the time, but they had insisted on having only Christian bands open for the concert. Though it was not promoted as such, it seemed that this was to be one of First Avenue's token "Christian" shows. The club had booked PFR and the 77's in previous years, but NLM was the first non-Nashville, non-CCM act they had ever booked. We weren't sure what the response would be like.

We had promoted the concert hard in the Christian scene, hoping that our numbers would be impressive and that we could actually raise some money for the rest of the world tour. We had passed out several hundred "comp" tickets[4] to people on the streets and around town earlier that week. And just across the river, the University of Minnesota was hosting a punk festival and we hoped some curious punks might wander in and check it out.

Unfortunately, the crowd was mostly Christians. I recognized a lot of faces from the local Christian colleges and from the New Union, Minneapolis' most popular live Christian music venue.

All three of the opening bands had been carefully selected from the current New Union scene, and I knew someone from every band playing. It never occurred to me what might happen, but as each band took the stage, it became obvious that their rehearsed antics and semantics were going to turn off just about every non-Christian in the club.

I can't say I blamed them. They just didn't know any better. The local Christian scene was just awash with bands that talked the talk, but kept their gigs neatly (or should I say, comfortably) aligned within the Christian community - churches, youth groups, camps, the New Union. The bands had pretty much been paralyzed by the condemning eyes of those

---

[4] i.e. complimentary

who might think they were playing music for the wrong reason or "watering down" their lyrics just to be "cool." I think I finally saw it for what it was: a shame game that keeps bands from reaching out of the Christian bubble and into the real world. And it was finally obvious that this was what had frustrated me all along about Christian music: Too much "preaching to the choir."

When NLM came on, I saw none of that. Here they were on the other side of the world playing in this important club in front of 600 people, and they didn't really care about the hype. They didn't care how many even came to the concert. They just cared about how many people heard the message and answered the call.

Sure at times, the rock opera looked like a souped-up Christian drama troupe - like what I would imagine a YWAM mime team does on the streets of Thailand or something - but, for the most part, it was stunning, it was daring and it was bold. No, I mean really *bold*. As a newspaper in Singapore would write later on in the tour, the rock opera had "lots of juicy bits. Like suicide. Physical abuse. Guns. Tarty blondes. Despair. A hunchbacked devil gleefully singing shock lyrics like 'rape, rape, rape. Celebrate your rape by your father!'"

It was a colorful and frenetic scene on the cramped stage. Even First Avenue's mainroom could not contain the wild spectacle that they called *Passion (an act of)*. Within minutes of its beginning, the crowd was literally entranced at the display of color and chaos. The story may have seemed a bit cliché, but the music behind it was interesting and the action on stage was intense.

Before the concert, we actually *prayed* together backstage, and the band invited the Holy Spirit to fill the place. They were completely humble, offering their talents and their desires to God. They didn't want to get in the way for God to move in a powerful way.

I realized that in all the years that I had been close to the Christian music scene, I had *never* prayed with any of my friends in Christian bands the way I prayed with NLM that night. It wasn't that my friends didn't pray. And it wasn't that my friends didn't try to be humble and offer their talents and their music to God. But there was something in the way NLM looked at this concert in First Avenue. They weren't proud that they were playing in such a "cool" club. They weren't even really glad to be playing with other Christian bands because it might make it more comfortable for them to be *Christians* in a very anti-Christian place. And it certainly wasn't another big show, and then on to the next city to sell more t-shirts.

The difference, to me, was in their attitude and their perspective.

They weren't out to prove anything to anybody. They didn't want to wow the crowd so they could sell CDs. In fact, they didn't want any attention on them. They only wanted to glorify God by proclaiming the name of Jesus. They had a higher calling. They had a purpose for playing that went beyond "making it bid" in music. They were above the little music circuit that every Christian band is locked into but they weren't self-righteous. They were just missionaries, *real* missionaries, carrying the Gospel via popular music (which happened to be grunge-metal, at the time), to young people around the world. It wasn't about the music. It was about the Message.

And when the story of the rock opera came to a close they had the audacity to make what they were talking about even more painfully obvious by singing a rock anthem if ever there was one: "God we thank you for sending us Jesus."

David Pierce spoke, as he often does at the end of NLM's performances, and invited people to come forward to know Jesus. It was hard to tell how many people responded, but about 15 people came forward for prayer. Some of the First Avenue staff may have mocked at the time, but two girls actually came forward because they saw one of the bartenders manifesting (shaking uncontrollably) because of the spiritual warfare being waged in the club that night. I, probably for the first time in my life, shared my faith with two teenagers backstage who wanted prayer for their messed up family situations. And members of Steiger Minneapolis were there to get to know the people who responded in order to follow-up on them.

It wasn't perfect, and it wasn't pretty. But it was powerful.

This, to me, was what the often-bandied-about term "music ministry" must *really* mean.

IN THE DAYS FOLLOWING THE CONCERT, we hurriedly finished packing our things and cleaning our apartment. We had mixed feelings about what we were getting ourselves into, but we were both sure that we wanted God's guidance and direction for our lives. Though we sometimes daydreamed about what it might be like to move to New Zealand and work with Steiger, we tried to keep out composure and simply say, *Enshallah*, God willing.

The hardest time for me was riding with my mother in her car to fetch some things from my parent's house. I can still see her, sitting at the red light, turning to me, tears in her eyes and she's crying, but not because she's sad that I'm going away. She's crying because she's so glad. "I just know you're in God's will," she says, beaming, crying. In God's will. That was how I felt. Like I had just stepped into this invisible tractor beam, and we were being sucked into this glorious River of Life.

The Burger King BBQ-bacon-cheeseburger I had consumed - my last supper in Minneapolis before the Reckoning - was still settling when the plane lifted off for Chicago, where we would catch a connecting flight to Frankfurt. The excitement of the moment and the short flight, soaring up and then soaring down, did wonders for me. The motion sickness I had had as a child came back to me, and two barf bags later, I was safely on the ground in Chicago, wondering what the rest of the flights ahead were going to be like.

We had flown ahead of the team to Chicago in order to arrange for the transport of the band's two large flight cases - which held props, costumes and equipment - to Frankfurt, shipping them "comat." When we had arranged the deal with the airline, we had assumed "comat" meant "free", because they were not charging us anything to ship the cases. Unfortunately, we found out later that "comat" meant "company materials" and that the cases would be the *last* things shipped on any given flight and *only* if there was enough room for them.

But we needed the flight cases in Germany for a concert we had in a few days, not to mention the concert we had the next day. It was the fourth of July and we were an hour too late when we arrived at the cargo office. The door was locked. The room was dark. We were pretty frustrated and concerned that the cases would be delayed for quite some time, and that we might not be able to fly ahead with the team if we had to stay behind and bring the cases.

We did some asking around, and fortunately, there was an off-duty customs official who just happened to be around. Strange. We went back, and sure enough, he met us at the closed office and was able to assist us. He swiftly stamped our legal papers, and we were informed that, yes, our flight cases - the two big-ugly-heavy ones - would be on the same exact flight as we were, booked from Chicago to Frankfurt.

And this is how I began to see God work. In everyday miracles. Things that seem like chance or coincidence. I knew better than that, but for some reason this seemed like the first time in my life that God was actually doing something obvious. First it was First Avenue, and now the cargo shipping. God was getting practical, and practically everywhere I looked I could see His fingerprints all over the good stuff.

Steve Knight and his wife, Becky, worked with Steiger International in the ministry's U.S. office, located in Northampton, Massachusetts.

AFTERWORD
by Floyd McClung

WHEN I FIRST MET DAVID PIERCE HE WAS A BROKEN AND DISCOURAGED MAN. He had been traveling around Europe trying to recover from being ripped off by some Christians in the States. His zeal for God was undiminished, but he was hesitant to get involved in working with more Christians, and he certainly was not anxious to join anyone else's bandwagon.

David had a lot of rough edges, and some people thought he'd never make it. He was too independent, they said. "The guy's crazy," said others. But though David was hesitant, and those around him doubtful, I saw within David Pierce the gift of an evangelist. I saw the spirit of a fierce warrior who would do anything for God. All he needed was a few people to believe in him and encourage him to go for it.

There are many people like that in the body of Christ. When they read books about well-known Christians, see them on stage, or watch them on television, many ordinary folk get the impression that God can never use them.

But that is not true!

God enjoys using ordinary people to do extraordinary things. Because then he gets the glory — at least if we will remember where we came from!

I am saying this to challenge you to believe God for the extraordinary. God sees in you the gifts and the calling that he placed within you. And if you will respond to his prompting to go for it, God will open a door for you.

David Pierce is still going for it. He is traveling all over the world reaching people with the gospel of Jesus Christ. When God looks around to find someone to fulfill a tough assignment and there's nobody radical enough to do it, he calls on David Pierce.

Are you radical enough to obey God and do anything that he asks you to do? Are you willing to step out and believe God for the impossible?

How about it? Are you going to accept your own personal invitation to the lions' den?

Floyd McClung is the former Executive Director of International Operations for Youth With A Mission (YWAM).

Evangelistic drama, Passion (an act of)

The Pierce's (Benjamin, Aaron, David & Jodi)

F.Y.I.

IF YOU WOULD LIKE MORE INFORMATION on how you can get involved with Steiger International or get copies of No Longer Music CDs please contact the Steiger office in your part of the world:

Steiger International U.S. Office P.O. Box 480 Huntington, MA 01050 USA	Toll Free: 888.827.1782 or Tel: 413.667.3471 Email: usa@steiger.org

Steiger International European Office Lessing Str. 36 D 76135 Karlsruhe Germany	Tel: 49.7218.306200 Fax: 49.7218.306299 Email: europe@steiger.org

Steiger International Australasia Office P.O. Box 13550 Waikanae New Zealand	Tel: 64.4.293.7721 Email: nz@steiger.org

Or visit us on the world-wide web at
www.steiger.org

AND JUST RELEASED...

Dancing with Skinheads & Other Bible Study Topics by David Pierce is a youth discipleship book to challenge young people to live radically for Jesus Christ. Contact us for a free copy.

ECFA MEMBER
The symbol of trust